Struggle for Power in Education

THE LIBRARY OF EDUCATION

A Project of The Center for Applied Research in Education, Inc.

G. R. Gottschalk, Director

Categories of Coverage

I	II	III
Curriculum and Teaching	Administration, Organization, and Finance	Psychology for Educators

IV	V	VI
History, Philosophy, and Social Foundations	Professional Skills	Educational Institutions

Struggle for Power in Education

FRANK W. LUTZ

JOSEPH J. AZZARELLI

Editors

Department of Administration and Supervision
School of Education
New York University

The Center for Applied Research in Education, Inc.
New York

Foreword

A new distribution of power is in the making in American public school systems. In many districts, teachers are pressing for and are gaining new power. Not only are they influencing educational policy, but they also are sharing in determining educational policy. No longer can the question be asked: should teachers have a more active role in determining policy? Currently, the question is: how *much* of a role should teachers have? Another question is: what policies should fall within the scope of teacher-superintendent-board negotiations? Some people would restrict such negotiations to the traditional area, that is, the economic rewards of teaching; others would impose hardly any restrictions at all on matters open to negotiation. Indeed, the current contract between the Board of Education of the City of New York and the United Federation of Teachers includes specific agreements concerning class size in the several kinds of schools, the length of the school day, the number of different rooms to which teachers may be assigned for their classes, and the kinds of duties teachers may be given when relieved of administrative assignments by school aides.

Teachers, in some cases, have been unable to secure desired working conditions when negotiating at the local level and have turned to the state legislatures using their political power there. As a result, school systems in seven states are now required by law to give teachers a duty-free lunch period. More fundamentally, in 1965, five states enacted legislation concerning professional negotiations which apply to school employees only. Five other states now have collective bargaining laws applicable to all public employees but with specific provisions applying to public school employees.

At a three-day conference in November, 1965, the Division of Administration and Supervision of the School of Education at New York University provided an opportunity for about 150 teachers, administrators, and school board members from three states to come together to consider and discuss the implications of the rising power of teacher organizations on education. The papers presented at that conference have been edited and are published in this volume of the Library of Education as a contribution to the growing literature on the problems of teacher-administrator-school board relations. The papers, as edited, present the problem of teacher power and then analyze it historically, sociologically, politically, economically, organizationally, and operationally. Descriptive material is interspersed with the theoretical analyses. This has been done in order to provide some new dimensions of description and to provide an explanation of intra-relationships in school districts which we are witnessing—or participating in—during the 1960's.

These analyses are hardly final answers. New thinking, new questions, new hypotheses, and, hopefully, new abilities to explain, describe, predict, and control the direction of the evolution will develop. Will the local teacher organization move over from the category of informal organization (or perhaps quasi-formal organization) to becoming a recognized part of the formal organization of schools? Will the aggressive activity of organized teacher groups lead to an enhanced or a diminished professionalization of teaching? How will the teachers' increasing sense of power affect the competition between their organizational and their professional commitments? Will a dichotomy develop, as Seymour Evans[1] suggests in a recent doctoral dissertation, wherein teachers will fall into two groups with diverse outlooks? One group would consist of teachers who hold a "sacred," school-marm, administration-oriented mind-set, embracing the "rural myth" of our society, accepting a non-rational affectivity, a familistic relationship, and a non-militant view of teacher collective behavior. Their outlook would set them off from a second group of teachers holding a "secular," new middle-class, bureaucratic, employee-oriented mind-set, embracing the new urban outlook of our society, accepting a rational goal direction, a functionally specific role dimension, a universalistic affectivity, a contractual relationship, and a militant view of teacher collective behavior. These questions illustrate that a new kind of thinking is needed which will lead to a new understanding, to new behaviors, new solutions, and, ultimately, to a new and better kind of educational environment. If effective, *Struggle for Power in Education* will generate that kind of thinking.

RICHARD C. LONSDALE, *Head*
Division of Administration and Supervision
School of Education
New York University

---

[1] *See* Seymour Evans, "Towards a Theory of Teacher Collective Organizational Behavior." (Unpublished doctoral dissertation, New York University, 1966.)

Contents

CHAPTER I

Four Viewpoints

JOSEPH J. AZZARELLI

School of Education, New York University

The emerging power of teacher organizations has had the illusion of a united purpose under a single banner, but, as in so many revolutions, this has tended to obscure the desires and anxieties that have motivated teachers to rally to "the cause." The following four statements attempt to delineate and clarify the causes that have impelled public school teachers to demand some sort of collective power.

School boards generally are opposed to the attempts of teacher unions to participate in educational decision-making believing that such attempts are contravening the constitutional prerogatives of the school board. The National School Boards Association recognizes that there are many areas of mutual concern but does not recognize that there is shared responsibility. Despite this adamant stand, school boards must face more state legislation in sharing decision-making responsibility and in participating in contract negotiations with teacher organizations. The legislature and the courts may no longer ignore these developments.

The American Federation of Teachers recognizes the axiom that all social systems alter their structure and processes as they accommodate to changes in their environment. It is this aspiration of accommodation that challenges the traditional stance of school board control of public education. The realities of the revolution of teacher power seem to be as David Selden describes and as Laurence Iannaccone predicts—that teacher organizations will continue to gain power. Legislative events in Connecticut, California, and Wisconsin indicate that school boards are not immovable objects.

In contrast to the school boards' stance of holding exclusive control over education, the National Education Association insists on the rights of teachers to participate with boards of education in formulating policies of common concern. This demand is not unlike that of the American Federation of Teachers. In fact, the two organizations

1

show striking similarities in their statements. Although the National Education Association prefers not to use union terms, such as "collective bargaining" and substitutes "professional negotiations" instead, an operational definition of each term reveals that there is little difference between them.

The real victim of the power struggle in education is the school administrator. Superintendent Santopolo realizes his executive role has diminished when teachers reject his efforts and proceed to deal directly with the school board on requests for salary changes and welfare improvement. His position is further diminished when the board, in turn, does not give him the responsibility and the authority to deal directly with teacher organizations. Without this power the school superintendent will find himself playing a decreasingly significant role in future negotiations. Frank Lutz identifies the superintendent's current role as that of a marginal man. Daniel Griffiths, on the other hand, suggests strongly that superintendents should be the authority responsible for the bargaining process.

A study of the four points of view[1] reveals a distinct battle line emerging: the militant teacher union on one side and the unyielding school boards on the other. The long established National Education Association, despite its protest, is essentially allied to the new power structure of the American Federation of Teachers, and, indeed, a merger of the two is a distinct possibility. On the side lines, forced to wait for a clear re-definition of his role, is the school superintendent.

School Board Viewpoint[2]

Board of education members are volunteer workers earnestly seeking to improve teacher compensation. It is small wonder that they are surprised and affronted when sudden demands are made by teachers with whom they feel allied. Board members recognize that the forces of change and growth, which characterize school board problems, also foster a new urgency among teachers who are concerned with their rights and responsibilities. The reaction to teacher power varies among school boards from those, on one extreme, who

---

[1] Statements for the following four viewpoints are digests of papers prepared for a Diamond Jubilee Conference considering "Problems of Teacher-School Board Relations—Implications of the Rising Power of Teacher Organizations" held November 7-10, 1965 by the Department of Administration and Supervision, School of Education, New York University.
The editors are responsible for editing the papers for publication.

[2] Summary of statement by Mrs. Ruth Page, Executive Secretary, New Jersey State Federation of District Boards of Education.

attach little importance to the militancy of teacher organizations, through those who have developed harmonious personnel policies, to those, on the other extreme, who are embroiled in disputes and threatened with strikes and sanctions.

A new dimension to the problem of school board-teacher relationships has evolved from the competition developing between two major organizations for the right to represent teachers' requests and grievances. While goals and procedures of the American Federation of Teachers and the National Education Association are basically the same, their rivalry is intense. The danger in this competition lies in the possibility that both the National Education Association and the American Federation of Teachers will make demands for benefits and exert pressures beyond the resources of the local boards. The goals of the organizations represent the teachers' desire for further status and for compensation befitting that status inasmuch as teachers have already achieved security, pensions, and many other benefits which are usually sought through such organizational action.

Board members believe that the goals of the teacher will infringe upon the board's legal prerogatives for decision making. In a policy statement on board-staff relationships, the National School Boards Association specifies that the decision-making responsibility of local boards may not be delegated and cannot be shared. Many boards will not recognize an organization which seeks to represent teachers because state legislation either expressly forbids it or does not specifically permit such recognition. Furthermore, boards believe that exclusive recognition of one teacher organization may not be granted because boards, as public bodies, must be open to the petitions of all. Although the legislative picture is changing yearly, boards in most states do not have the legislative right to negotiate with teachers and enter collective bargaining agreements, and they do not feel the need for such legislation. Most school boards meet with their teachers, hear their requests, and strive toward reaching agreements acceptable to the teachers within the limits of local resources and in accordance with procedures already effective in the districts.

The most controversial goal of a teacher organization is the right of appeal to a third party in the event of an impasse in a prolonged disagreement. Boards vigorously oppose proposals for legislation which require submitting the appeal to a third party. They base this on the grounds that decisions on board policy must be made by persons legally responsible to the electorate and that decisions made by other agencies allow for a gradual "outside" control over public education in place of local control. Such legislation could disenfranchise the voters of the district.

Boards reject the use of strikes and sanctions by teacher groups as illegal and as inimical to the educational welfare of children. In the interest of better education, therefore, the school boards should try to prevent the teachers from taking such drastic action by taking the initiative themselves in determining teacher needs and then by cooperatively formulating policies to meet these needs. Such action should be consistent with professional dignity and within the available resources of the community. School boards feel that it would be unfortunate to apply to the profession of public teaching the same procedures followed by labor. The vast differences between public and private employment render unsuitable to public service procedures that are suitable to private enterprise. Education is basically a public trust concerned with the welfare of children; it has no profit to share, hence there should be no profit-making motive. Board and staff do share common goals in the responsibility for public education.

Traditionally, boards have operated in a policy-making role and have assumed that a satisfactory professional relationship exists between administration and staff. Board members fear that teacher demands to negotiate directly with local boards will undermine the authority of superintendents and will bypass regular channels of communication, thus intimidating administrators. Furthermore, school board members feel that school system decisions could conceivably be made by teacher organizations anxious to promote interests other than the educational interests of the children.

Board members must face their responsibilities clearly and realistically and regard as ineffective the ultra-conservative, the provincial, and the politically motivated elements of their membership. It is time for the National School Boards Association and the state school board associations to offer leadership in encouraging local boards to up-grade their membership and to revise policies which no longer meet school needs. When perspective becomes lost in local problems, when boards and teachers are unable to agree upon their respective roles, then the state school board associations should be prepared to play major roles by offering insight and objectivity in resolving the issues.

Teacher demands for a greater role in policy making will have considerable effect on the future of lay control of education. School boards feel that teacher demands for increased power cannot be permitted to lessen or destroy the legal power of the local board because the American system of education would lose much of the strength and diversity it has obtained from lay control. In the present changing society, board members agree that the system of checks and balances which lay control brings to professional influence are needed more than ever before.

Beset with many other insurmountable problems, local school boards were unprepared during the first stage of the teachers' bid for power—the initiative was seized by the teachers, where it remains. Efforts to formalize board-staff relationships are moving into a second stage—teachers are refining and working toward their goals through legislative mandate whereby procedures will be evolved allowing them to participate in discussions on matters which directly affect them. Boards feel that there must be a proper balance between lay and professional participation in policy development. School boards can now restore this balance if they will move quickly with new proposals which will ultimately lead to effective policies for harmonious relationships.

In defending their opposition to legislative proposals made by teacher associations and unions, school boards maintain that restrictive or mandatory legislation which weakens decision-making powers can be as destructive to education as strikes and sanctions. They also take the stand that unilateral action by teachers is as detrimental to educational progress as unilateral action by boards of education, and neither should be tolerated.

If balance is to be effected in board-staff relationships, efforts must not stop with the examination and improvement of board policies only. Teachers, too, need to reassess their goals realistically. Teachers cannot afford to seek power for its own sake, nor can they afford to limit concerns to their own welfare. The new concept of the full meaning of the great American dream—education of each child to his fullest ability—demands much more time, talent, and resources than has been allotted previously to public education. Demands limited only to teacher welfare, while they may lead to better conditions for teachers, do not necessarily add to the improvement of programs for children (e.g., teacher welfare gains do not directly reduce the number of dropouts nor raise the level of pupil achievement). School boards feel that teacher organizations have not made true professional improvement a major goal, that such organizations must find ways to up-grade members so that those accepting the benefits of tenure will correspondingly accept responsibility for a continued high level of achievement, and that such teacher organizations must emphasize professional improvement in order to merit the respect and consideration of the board and the public represented by the board.

All issues should be decided in terms of the educational needs of the children, the general welfare of teachers, the proper balance of administrative control, the legal responsibility of the board, and the available resources of the community. In general, school boards feel that nothing can take the place of a climate of mutual confidence in which both board and staff recognize that their common interests are greater than their differences. Legislation will not avoid the bitterness which comes when either board or staff seeks action unilaterally. Appeals to third parties, following prolonged disputes, often result in public opinion that ignores or misunderstands the full issues involved; an alienated public will not support its schools.

Effective local control recognizes that public education is the single most important function of a democracy. It calls for capable leadership, public support, dedicated teachers, and reasonable solutions to board-staff problems. It would eliminate political control and provincialism from local boards. Effective local control encourages boards to act for the greatest good of the community and for the best interests of the school in serving the needs of the greater society.

American Federation of Teachers Viewpoint[3]

There is no doubt that the relationship between teachers, on one hand, and administration, boards of education, and society itself, on the other, is in an accelerated process of evolution. American education is in the midst of a dynamic readjustment of traditional power and status relationships which may continue for a number of years until a new equilibrium is reached. The American Federation of Teachers is striving to achieve a more favorable position for teachers.

The motive power behind the education revolution is the new teacher militancy. Avoiding the stigma of the word "militancy," the American Federation of Teachers prefers to think of "militancy" as caring enough about solving a problem to do something about it

[3] Summary of statement by Mr. David Selden, Assistant to the President, American Federation of Teachers.

without undue concern for one's personal reward. The new militancy of teachers was episodic and formless until New York City teachers hit upon collective bargaining as their central, unifying objective. The theory of collective bargaining has been constantly refined since 1935, but the basic idea remains: employees as a group have a right to bargain with management as to the terms and conditions under which they will perform their work. For today's militant teachers, the collective bargaining concept has the classic unifying force of "the idea whose time has come."

Before 1960, the American Federation of Teachers was not taken seriously by the educational establishment which was dominated by the National Education Association. Federation literature began talking about collective bargaining as early as 1955, but few of its members understood the idea involved. Some local unions had achieved positions of power in their school districts and other locals were gaining power, but their stance was largely defensive. In 1960, when the New York City teachers turned to the militant Local No. 2 of the American Federation of Teachers for leadership, the National Education Association was forced to sit up and take notice.

The drive of teachers for increased power shows no sign of abating; it will continue to affect the traditional establishment. The victory of the American Federation of Teachers in New York City touched off a new wave of militancy both inside and outside the Federation. As a result of the new impetus, Detroit, Cleveland, Boston, and Philadelphia teachers have chosen the Federation as their exclusive representative. More significant than winning more city elections is the fact that an increasing number of representation elections will be held, regardless of who wins. Inevitably a competition between contracts will develop which will compel the education associations to become more and more like unions. On the other hand, there are almost no forces moving the American Federation of Teachers to become less militant. The collective bargaining dynamic is all the other way.

In essence, professionalism is one's responsibility for exercising independent action and making expert judgment while performing one's work. The traditional paternalistic system in education stands squarely in opposition to the true professional status for teachers; as teachers seek professionalism, they seek to counteract the paternal role of school authorities which has influenced policy making in education for the past century. Collective bargaining fits neatly into this situation because it provides the means for teachers to exercise their collective judgment and to establish a much larger zone of individual professional authority.

Bargaining agents of the American Federation of Teachers have already negotiated such matters as maximum class sizes, staffing ratios, teaching hours, after school programs, assignments of teachers to class programs, transfers within the school system, and the assignment of teachers to non-classroom chores. All were once considered entirely within the authority of the superintendent and the school board. In addition to the areas listed above, the Federation foresees that, in a short time, teachers will negotiate hiring standards and innovate experimental and research projects involving the entire educative process.

Peculiarly enough, there is little disagreement regarding objectives between teachers and administrators, or between teachers and those school board members who serve because their interest lies in education rather than in the tax rate. Everybody wants better schools. The disagreement comes in the authority area—*who* will make the decisions.

If the beginning of teacher power is teacher militancy, then its effective mechanism is collective bargaining, but there is a solid rule in negotiations that what one gains at the bargaining table is directly proportional to the power one brings to the bargaining table (no school system has even moved toward collective bargaining until the teachers have made a show of power). The word "power" is taboo in education, but teachers have finally begun to talk about society and government in terms of the complex of power-relationships which are the realities of social dynamics.

In a magazine article last May, David Selden maintained that the strike is the most professional and the most effective means for exerting teacher power. He said:

> Where the right—and the willingness—to strike exists, most disputes will be settled without an actual walkout. . . . There are four alternatives to the strike, and all are much worse than a possible work stoppage. Disputes can be "settled" by: (1) continuing the status quo; (2) carrying on a cold war between teachers and school authorities; (3) political action; or (4) arbitration. The first, . . . the "don't complain" philosophy, is unthinkable if we really want good education. The second . . . erodes morale and seldom results in any real solution to the problems confronting the school. . . . Frequently the choice of opposing candidates offers little hope for

improvement. . . . [Finally,] neither side will bargain if it knows that the dispute is going to wind up in the hands of an arbitrator.[4]

Two additional problems involved in teacher power are (1) the legal restrictions against strikes, and (2) the possible abuses of teacher power. Many states have laws forbidding strikes by public employees. Most judges will grant injunctions against such strikes. In courts, the power resides with the employer, particularly a public employer (e.g., school boards) which is deemed to possess sovereign powers derived from the state. Except in a few very large cities, the out-and-out strike is not a reliable source of power, although it is useful as a protest. Variations on the mass resignation theme and other forms of work stoppages have been extremely effective. If a *group* of employees resigns, the employer is then forced to replace each one—a difficult thing when skilled professional teachers are involved—or to negotiate the terms of that group's return to work.

Probably the best solution to the work stoppage problem is a "no-contract, no-work" policy. Shortly after the first New York City contract in 1962 (following a one-day strike), the United Federation of Teachers adopted the resolution: "Henceforth New York City teachers will render their services only under the terms and conditions of a collective bargaining contract." The no-contract, no-work principle will likely be extended, with strikes implementing the no-work policy in large cities, and mass resignations in small districts. Other sources of teacher power include public relations, research, and the support of affiliated organizations all of which are auxiliary aids rather than major sources of support.

Until the last two decades almost all power has resided in the board of education and the administrators. A new equilibrium would involve a sharing of power and a consequent greater professionalization of teachers. All will benefit—students and the general public as well as those who make education a career. When teachers wage a successful fight for smaller classes, everyone benefits. When staffing ratios are improved, everyone in education can do a more professional job. When teachers' salaries are raised, school boards and administrators can be more selective in their employment policies.

The old educational establishment has found itself unable to cope with the demands of modern society. The 1965 White House Con-

---

[4] David Selden, "Needed: More Teacher Strikes," *Saturday Review,* May 15, 1965, p. 75.

ference on Education was an "over the top" effort to break away from the restrictions of the establishment, just as the new teacher movement represents a similar effort at the grass roots level. School board members and administrators can help prevent a new period of stultification in educational policy by granting teachers a seat at the bargaining table. What happens after that will depend upon the give and take of negotiations. Out of the sharing of ideas, the mutual respect on which the new relationship must be based, can come a new era of educational progress.

New York State Teachers Association Viewpoint[5]

Teachers, along with the legally constituted board of education, share a joint responsibility for the maintenance of an educational system sufficient to meet the needs of a free society. The state teachers associations [and the National Education Association, ed.] approach to the problem is predicated upon the acceptance of this shared responsibility. In a policy statement adopted by its board of directors, the New York State Teachers Association declared: "We insist on the right of teachers, through democratically selected representatives using professional channels, to participate with boards of education in the formulation of policies of common concern, including matters relating to compensation and other conditions of professional service."

To implement this policy, the state association has submitted recent legislation requiring school authorities to provide their teachers with the definite opportunity to meet with school authorities to be heard and to make recommendations concerning school district policies. They want the right to do this through the representatives of their own choice. Legislation establishes that it shall be the duty of both the school authorities and the teachers to attempt, in good faith, to reach agreement concerning such policies. It further requires the Board of Regents to establish procedures for impartial *review* of serious disagreements which may arise between school authorities and teachers. Such legislation has been strongly opposed by the New York State School Boards Association, but last year the school boards association adopted a resolution urging member boards to give their professional staff the

---

[5] Summary of statement by Dr. G. Howard Goold, Executive Secretary, New York State Teachers Association.

opportunity to be heard and the occasion to consult with boards on matters of school policy affecting teachers as a professional group and as individuals.

Representing teachers, the education association must understand what the teachers really want. Basically, teachers need to know where they stand. They desire a better definition of their role in the hierarchy of the American school system. They want acceptance as working equals, equality of status, and recognition of their competencies in their own area of responsibility. They do not intend to take over management of the schools, but they do want to feel that their recommendations are sought and heeded in simple matters as, for instance, the selection of a textbook. They would like to feel that in the matters where they have a legitimate concern, their advice and counsel would be accepted in the same manner a board of education would accept the counsel of its attorney, architect, or business agent. Putting it more bluntly, they do not want to be talked down to but they do want to be talked to at eye-level. Teachers are better prepared than ever before. In the dignity of their professional competence they do not appreciate being directed in every detail of their daily function.

Since the close of World War II with the tremendous influx of young men into the teaching ranks at all levels, an impatience with the status quo has resulted in a determination to do something about changing it. These men want to assume a more active role in the formulation of school policies.

In New York, as well as in other states, the state teachers association has become the dominant professional group for their own improvement. Through several legislatures, the Association took action to raise minimum school standards. It lobbied to establish retirement systems and minimum salary protection for teachers. While pressing efforts to pursue educational betterment through the state legislature, the New York State Teachers Association has made a strong commitment to the concept of maintaining *local* control and keeping autonomy within school districts.

Finally, the National Education Association cannot and must not ignore the impact that the trade unions are having in their all-out attempt to organize the teachers at the local level. Since World War II the interest of unions in organizing teachers has been steadily increasing. The competition for teachers' loyalties will continue as a major interest for some time. Some of the problems that the educational field is now facing among teachers have been precipitated by this head-on competition with trade unionism and by the existence of two organizational groups. Whether the term is "collective bargaining" or "professional negotiations," the New York State Teachers Association remains unconvinced that the collective bargaining approach provides the best solution to giving school personnel participation in the formulation of educational policy.

Education associations are hopeful—and they strongly believe—that among school board members, school administrators, and classroom teachers, the potential exists for finding ways to bring all concerned into a mutual resolution of present disagreements and to redefine the proper role of teachers in shaping educational policy. In this day of "bigness," with school districts becoming ever larger, boards and administrators will have to work with and through duly constituted teacher organizations. With such numbers involved, organizations will of necessity have to accept full responsibility for their actions.

Superintendent Viewpoint[6]

Superintendents of schools view the problem of teacher power from a dual vantage point. As administrators, they look upon teachers with sincere respect and admiration for the significant contribution they make to society as a whole. As former classroom teachers, most superintendents still look back fondly to the satisfactions and joys experienced as teachers.

Examining the power of teachers today, superintendents see two major sources from which it emanates: the power of the individual teacher, and the collective power of the group. The power of the individual teacher has always been an important force in American culture, but in the last twenty years teachers as a group have undergone a considerable change. Although the rights and privileges of individuals should always remain inviolate, history has shown that unity is the key to social power. Teachers are now coming together to strengthen their role in American life. It is quite startling to envision one unified group of people (teachers) having so much educational knowledge and intellectual power. This new power could conceivably become the strongest single human force in our country and in our time.

Problems experienced in the exercise of teacher power are prob-

[6] Summary of statement by Dr. Michael V. Santopolo, Superintendent of Schools, Union Free School District No. 14, Hewlett, New York.

lems encountered in any new pattern of relationships. On the one hand, there is the insistent manner in which teachers are striving to participate in the affairs of management. This is augmented, on the other hand, by the restive manner board members seek to maintain and protect what they consider to be their legal responsibilities and prerogatives. This is further complicated by the often insecure manner in which the superintendent tries to maintain his strategic position as chief executive of the board of education, leader of the professional staff, and chief administrative guardian of the schools, the educational programs, and the children of the community.

Teachers have been participating in the management of school affairs all along, but this participation has been indirect, sporadic, and for the most part unrecognized. The current press for recognition, direct participation, and for the right to be seated at the management table has created difficulties. Teachers often approach the situation with desperate aggressiveness, impatient desire for rapid progress, and extreme sensitivity to the possibility of being rebuffed. These factors, together with the inexperience of all parties striving for a new pattern of relationships, often contribute to misunderstandings. Teacher representatives tend to distrust the superintendent. Sometimes they do not understand the difference between having a role in decision making and actually making the decision. Very often teachers have no time to spare and lack careful preparation. Often a faculty is unable to select its very best representatives for one reason or another. Consequently, teachers' efforts are sometimes characterized by inept approaches at crucial moments, thus defeating carefully nurtured groundwork. Teachers may tend to brush aside the superintendent in their rush to do battle with the board directly. After reaching the board, they sometimes make light of the responsibilities, limitations, and commitments that board members and superintendents must assume by virtue of the legal and moral trust which the community has placed on them. Teacher representatives may be so preoccupied with their immediate purpose that the long term welfare of the pupil, school, community, and even their own colleagues may be sacrificed. Such action is inevitably viewed as irresponsible and justifies the criticism made that such teachers are not yet ready to share management efforts.

The superintendent also contributes his share of mistakes to these relationships. Generally speaking, he falls into one of three categories as he reacts to teacher power: (1) he may refuse to recognize the existence of a problem, (2) he may admit the problem exists but may not admit that it affects his district, or (3) he may recognize that teacher power can be used constructively. The latter is the best approach for today's superintendent to take toward the problem of teacher power. Not only is it morally right to welcome teachers to the consultation table, but it is practical and strategic to do it *now!*

Teacher power, as it grows and is sometimes exercised, becomes a tremendous threat to the superintendent of schools. Superintendents are being bypassed by the teachers, and their efforts are being rejected. Teachers proceed directly to the school board with their requests for salary changes and welfare improvements. Local teacher associations often claim credit for changes which the superintendent and members of the board have helped to design. However, the superintendent must view the situation realistically: teacher power is here to stay!

Many districts have already found solutions through jointly developed agreements. Local, state, and national associations of teachers, board members, and administrators are focusing their efforts and resources toward constructive solutions. Institutions of higher learning recognize the significance of this problem and wish to lend their efforts and energies constructively.

As a legally constituted elective body, the board of education is responsible to the electorate and is morally responsible for decisions to all the people involved—pupils, parents, teachers, and citizens. Board members are relatively powerless to become involved; they have no right to act or even to react except as a board of trustees. Furthermore, much of the responsibility involved in contacts between teachers and authorities is administrative; thus, the responsibility falls into the hands of the superintendent, who is the executive officer of the board and the chief administrative officer of the district. Board members, holding voluntary, unpaid positions, cannot give all of their time, energy, and effort to school affairs; hence, the superintendent and his administrative staff must assume the primary role.

Superintendents in New York City recognize the need for change and have become involved in constructive efforts. A committee of the New York State Council of Village and City School Superintendents has a three-fold purpose in one such effort: (1) to bring together the executive leadership of all parties concerned and the commissioner's representatives in an effort to settle differences and to develop constructive approaches at the seat of executive power, (2) to assist the State Education Department in preparing a guide for the use of local districts, and (3) to encourage the State Education Department to lend its constructive assistance and aggressive leadership to this effort, and to consider ways in which the department itself may be constructively involved in this new power structure. The work of this committee perhaps best summarizes the superintendent's view of teacher power today. He is willing to help develop a new pattern of relationships. He looks forward to working with teachers in a carefully planned, well-organized structure. In this perspective, the superintendent no longer sees teacher power as a problem. He sees it as a blessing!

CHAPTER II

The History of the Fight to Control Policy in Public Education

RAYMOND E. CALLAHAN

Graduate Institute of Education, Washington University

The most important fact about the American public school system, relevant to policy determination, is that it has been characterized by extreme decentralization. The federal government has not played an active role in public education until recently and the states, which have the legal power and responsibility for providing and controlling education, have for the most part delegated this power to local authorities. There have been times in our history when strong state commissioners have acted vigorously to support, control, and direct public education but, for the most part, the states have done nothing more than establish broad legal frameworks and provide for financial support. They left the major responsibility for establishing and maintaining schools to the local officials in thousands of school districts all over the country. The pattern was established in colonial Massachusetts and has spread across the country.

Until recently, the struggle to determine policy within schools has been primarily a struggle between school boards and superintendents —teachers have not been involved. And although at times the struggle has broken into the open and become a public fight, for the most part it has been conducted quietly, behind the closed doors of school board meeting rooms. What was the nature of this struggle; why and how was it conducted? Why have teachers not been involved until recent years? The answers to both these questions lie in the unique way the American system of public schools was established in the first place and in the way it developed over time.

Lay Committees

In the beginning, the power to establish, control, and manage schools was placed in the hands of lay committees. These lay committees raised revenues, hired and fired teachers, decided on text-

books and school programs, and examined pupils. When the popula‑
tion of the country was small, and before schools were made both
free and compulsory, this system apparently worked fairly well. But
in the 1830's and 1840's free public elementary schools were
established in state after state. Gradually attendance in them was
made compulsory. At the same time the country entered a period of
tremendous population growth which has continued down to the
present time. It was not simply a matter of population growth but
also a matter of change—change from a simple agrarian society to a
complex industrial one. From roughly 1840 on, with each year that
passed, there have been more students to be educated, the *need* to
educate them has been greater, and the nature of the educational
effort has become more complex.

As the educational and administrative task became more com‑
plex, community leaders responded in one of two ways: (1) to
increase the size of the school committee and/or divide the city into
districts with a separate committee managing the school or schools
within each district, or (2) to hire a person to do the work. Thus the
office of the city superintendent of schools was created.

Boston school committee. One event dramatically illustrating
the inadequacy of the system of management by lay committees,
which indicated the need for the creation of the superintendency
and which undoubtedly hastened its establishment, was the "Survey"
made by some members of the Boston school committee in 1845.
The background of the "Survey" was this: Horace Mann had been
appointed commissioner of education in Massachusetts in 1837. In
the spring of 1843, Mann visited Europe. He was greatly impressed,
especially by the Prussian schools, with their warmth and their excit‑
ing intellectual qualities. Mann's account of his observations was
published in his now famous *Seventh Annual Report 1843*. The
contrast between the Prussian schools and the Massachusetts schools,
including the Boston schools, with their harshness and ineffective‑
ness, was vivid indeed. As a result throughout 1844 Mann was in‑
volved in a running battle of rejoinders to rejoinders with a group of
Boston schoolmasters.[1] This controversy led public education into
becoming a burning issue, especially in Boston.

In order to get some evidence which might provide a basis for
settling the question of who was right, some members of the Boston

---

[1] Lawrence A. Cremin, ed., *Horace Mann, The Republic and the School* (New
York: Bureau of Publications, Teachers College, Columbia University, 1957),
p. 54.

School Committee decided to devote time and energy in studying the actual conditions of the public schools in their city. The studies were made at the end of the school year—1845—and the Report was issued in August. Long extracts of the contents of the Report were published by Horace Mann (as editor) in the *Common School Journal*. Commenting editorially on the Report, Horace Mann stated[2] that it had "filled the intelligent citizen of Boston . . . with amazement and grief" and had "spread through the city a general and deep feeling of sorrow and mortification." He felt that it would be "sad indeed" if these reactions "should die away without producing a reform."

Why were the schools of Boston in such a state? The Committee placed the blame directly on the administrative arrangements for the school system and it recommended reforms—the most important of which was the appointment of a superintendent of schools. According to the Committee, the basic problem was that the schools were being run by a school board of twenty-four men who were not paid for their labor and who "share a responsibility, which thus broken into fragments, presses on no one."[3] Furthermore, there was the question of the school board members themselves, "who must, on the common principle of human nature, be supposed to be made willing to hold this office by every variety of motive, from the highest and purest love of usefulness, down to a mere personal purpose of coining its privileges and opportunities into dollars and cents."[4]

The Committee did not propose to eliminate the school board. On the contrary, they believed that "for some purposes" it was "admirable." Its members were "fresh from the people, every year; and being chosen from all the wards, they represent all the wants and interests which should be provided for, and all the opinions and feelings which should be consulted." They would keep these "excellent elements" but add those which were "wholly wanting" and these "wanting" elements were *permanence, personal responsibility, and continued and systematic labor*."[5] To achieve this end they would appoint a new official—a superintendent of schools.

Despite the devastating criticism resulting from the investigation, and despite the school board's request for funds which would enable them to appoint a superintendent, the Common Council of the city

---

[2] Horace Mann in *Common School Journal*, VII, No. 20 (October, 1845), pp. 344–345.

[3] *Ibid.*, p. 310.

[4] *Ibid.*

[5] *Ibid.*, p. 309 (Author's italics).

voted against the proposal. A superintendent was not appointed in Boston until six years later—1851. Even then he was not given needed authority. Apparently this was true in other cities as well in those early years. Ellwood P. Cubberley, commenting on how small the number of city superintendencies were that had been established before 1870, states that those which were established had limited authority and that the school boards had "assigned clerical rather than executive functions to the new official."[6] Evidence indicates that the unwillingness of school boards to confer authority upon their new officials continued throughout the nineteenth century. For example, William A. Mowry, a prominent educator who had been a superintendent of schools and also a member of the school board in Boston for many years at the end of the century, wrote a long article on school administration in 1895. He concluded with these remarks:

> The conclusion cannot but be evident that the school regulations of Boston place practically the whole executive power used in carrying on the public schools of that city in the hands of the standing committees of the school board. The superintendent and supervisors do not exercise this power, because it is not lodged in their hands.
>
> I have purposely outlined the condition of affairs in Boston, because Boston is not only the metropolis of New England, but is a typical city in regard to its school management. What is true of Boston in relation to these matters is substantially true of other New England cities.[7]

Even though by 1895 there was widespread agreement that the superintendent of schools was a desirable and even necessary official in a school system (for practically every city and an increasing number of smaller communities had actually appointed and were paying such a person), he had in most cases been given very little authority.

School Board–Superintendent Conflict of 1895

The struggle between school boards and superintendents broke into open battle in 1895. It was probably the boldest attack ever made by administrators as a group upon school boards. If it had succeeded, American education would have been far different in the twentieth century. The basic issue in the conflict was: who would run the schools? When the smoke had cleared, it was obvious that, while

---

6 Ellwood P. Cubberley, *Public School Administration* (Boston: Houghton-Mifflin Co., 1916), p. 58.

7 William A. Mowry, "Powers and Duties of School Superintendents," *Educational Review*, IX, (January, 1895), p. 44.

the superintendents had made significant gains, they had not won a clear-cut victory. A compromise settlement was worked out. In principle at least, some agreement was reached between both groups on several of the major issues; but on some others there was disagreement and subsequent failure to solve basic problems.

Background. Why did the battle erupt in 1895; how was it fought and by whom? As far as the timing is concerned, it was greatly influenced by the work of Joseph Mayer Rice. Rice had been trained as a physician and had gone to Germany in the late 1880's for additional study. While he was there, he got interested in education, took some work in pedagogy, and visited in some German schools. He maintained his interest in education after returning to the United States and in 1892 made an extensive study of the public schools. Between January and June of that year, Rice observed more than twelve hundred teachers in schools in thirty-six cities. He also attended school board meetings and spoke with superintendents and principals. His findings as well as his recommendations were published in the *Forum* magazine between October, 1892 and June, 1893. He reported that the schools which he had visited were, with few exceptions, in miserable shape. Rice believed there were many factors responsible for this situation but one of the pertinent ones (and the one germane to this topic) was that the schools were operated by school boards. In some places, he said, board members used the schools for their own selfish or political gain. In others, they thought of themselves as educators and actually tried to run the schools. He urged that the operation of the schools be turned over to competent educators. To achieve this end he thought it would be necessary for Americans to rouse themselves to elect good school board members who, in turn, would select a competent superintendent. The board would then give the new official "a sufficient amount of independent power to enable him to improve the schools in any manner that may to him seem fit."[8]

---

[8] Joseph Mayer Rice, *The Public School System of the United States* (New York: Century Co., 1893), p. 19. There is no doubt that, given the incompetence and corruption of school board members, sooner or later efforts at reform would have been made. And given the increasing size and complexity of the educational system, sooner or later school board members would have had to have turned the educational job over to educators. But in either case, educators, and especially school administrators, would probably have had to take action and to take action they would probably have had to have been aroused. There is no way of telling how long it would have taken for the frustration of school administrators to build up to the point where they would act. Rice started it and he may have been the original "muck-raking" journalist. Even one of his loudest critics, A. E. Winship, editor of the *Journal of Education* had to admit that Rice had "encouraged the

The first of Rice's articles on conditions in the city schools appeared in October, 1892; the last in June, 1893. In the first article he criticized school boards and offered recommendations for strengthening the superintendency. In February, 1893—three months later —a committee of prominent school administrators was appointed by the Department of Superintendence of the National Education Association with the purpose of studying and making recommendations on three problems: (1) the correlation of studies, (2) the training of teachers, and (3) the organization of city school systems. This became the "famous" Committee of Fifteen. The committee was divided into three sub-committees of five men each. The sub-committee on the organization of city school systems had as chairman Andrew S. Draper, superintendent of schools in Cleveland. In February, 1895 it reported to the N.E.A. Perhaps Draper would have been appointed in any case, but it seems significant that he was one of the schoolmen praised by Rice.[9] By the time its 1894 meeting was called, the Committee had developed a set of questions to guide each sub-committee in its work. The questions presented to Draper's committee show something about the nature of the problems educators faced. They also are proof that these were not timid, cautious men. They were not afraid to ask basic questions—very first question on the list indicates this. Following are the questions they raised:

> *Should there be a board of education, or a commissioner with an advisory council?*
>
> If a commissioner, should he be elected by the people, or appointed by the mayor, or selected in some other way?
>
> What should be his powers and duties?
>
> If a board of education, of how many members should it consist? Should the members be elected or appointed? From the city at large or to represent districts?
>
> By what authority should the superintendent of schools be elected or appointed? and for what term?
>
> Should the city superintendent owe his appointment directly or in-

---

educational reformers of several cities to organization and effort." (Vol. **XLIV,** August, 1896, p. 128). He made educators and the country aware of the nature and extent of the problem. And he helped create a climate in which change, even dramatic change, might be possible. School administrators took advantage of that climate and gradually were able to change their situation for the better, and if it had not been for one man they might have achieved a dramatic total victory in their struggle with school boards.

[9] *Ibid.,* p. 227.

directly to the state educational authorities and be responsible to
them rather than to the local authorities?

In whom should be vested the power to appoint teachers? In whom
the power to discharge teachers?

By whom should the course of study be made?

By whom should textbooks be selected?

By whom should promotions be made? [10]

In its report the Committee did not recommend the elimination of
school boards but it came very close to it, especially when it strongly
endorsed the Cleveland Plan.[11] The recommendations, if they had
been followed, would virtually have turned the schools over to the
superintendent and his staff.

The Committee believed that administrative duties "naturally and
quickly" separated themselves into two great departments: "one
which manages the business offices and the other which supervises
the instruction." These departments should be headed by full-time
persons and the head of the instructional staff had to be a "competent educational expert." In both departments there had to be "adequate authority and quick public accountability." The Committee
then stressed the need to discriminate between the legislative and the
executive functions in organizing and administering the schools. The
legislative function should be handled by a small board appointed by
the mayor of the city. Its job would be to determine and direct the
general policy of the school system. It should have power to levy
taxes, raise revenue, and control expenditures but should make no
appointments in the business department "other than its own clerk."
The entire operation should be "absolutely emancipated from partisan politics and completely dissociated from municipal business."
So far as the instructional side was concerned, the Committee recommended a superintendent be appointed by the board and that
"once appointed he should be independent." He should have full

---

[10] N.E.A. *Proceedings* (1895), pp. 234–235 (Author's italics).

[11] The editor of *The American School Board Journal* printed the following
description of the Plan which had been published in a "Handbook of the Cleveland
Board of Education."

"On March 18, 1892, the General Assembly of Ohio passed an act providing
for the reorganization of the board of education of Cleveland. Under this act all
legislative authority is vested in a school council of *only* seven members at large,
and *all executive authority* is vested in a school director. The school director ap-
points all subordinates. The *Superintendent* of instruction is appointed by the
school director, and may be removed by him for cause. The Superintendent of
instruction shall have the *sole charge to appoint and discharge* all assistants and
teachers authorized by the council to be employed." This was followed by a strong
editorial criticism of the Plan. Vol. XI (December, 1895), p. 10.

power to select his staff; hire, fire, and promote teachers; and have complete control over the educational program. The question remained, however, how were these arrangements to be brought about since it was certain that at least some school board members would not relinquish their power willingly. The Committee stated that this power could be "secured in the law." It further added that it must be secured in this way "or it will not be secured at all." Finally, the Committee recommended that the superintendent of instruction be "given a long term"—they suggested a term of from five to ten years.[12]

The Committee did not content itself with strong positive recommendations—it also criticized school boards in very strong language.

> It [school system] is administration by boards or committees, the members of which are not competent to manage professional matters and develop an expert teaching-force. Yet they assume, and in most cases honestly, the knowledge of the most experienced. *They override and degrade a superintendent, when they have the power to do so, until he becomes their mere factotum. For the sake of harmony and the continuance of his position he concedes, surrenders, and acquiesces in their acts, while the continually increasing teaching-force becomes weaker and weaker and the work poorer and poorer. If he refuses to do this, they precipitate an open rupture and turn him out of his position. Then they cloud the issues and shift the responsibility from one to another. There are exceptions, of course, but they do not change the rule.*[13]

On the basis of all the evidence available, and there is considerable evidence in both the professional and lay journals, this statement was certainly justifiable—it described the true situation existing in the schools in 1895. But strategically it probably was a mistake since it antagonized school board members in general and one in particular. That man was William George Bruce, both school board member and founder and editor of the *American School Board Journal* who led the fight against the superintendents. He was an able, powerful adversary—more powerful because he had a journal at his disposal.

Open conflict.   Bruce was a Milwaukee newspaperman who had been elected to the school board in that city. In 1891, he decided there was a need for a journal to serve school board members, so he

---

[12] N.E.A. *Proceedings* (1895), pp. 375–389. Most of these ideas did not originate with this committee; they had been discussed by educators occasionally after 1890 and they had actually been put into effect in Cleveland in the spring of 1892. The Cleveland Plan was cited frequently in the Report naturally since Draper had been superintendent there from 1892 to 1894.

[13] *Ibid.*, p. 382 (Author's italics).

founded one. Through this journal he informed board members and superintendents about what was going on around the country. He included all kinds of educational matters from the latest ventilating systems to use to what new books on teaching methods were available. Through his editorial page he spoke directly to board members and superintendents, presenting very definite ideas on how he thought the schools should be run and who should run them.

Important is the fact that he was both the great advocate and the defender of school boards. It is impossible to estimate exactly the extent of the influence Bruce exerted either through his journal or his other activities but it was considerable. As owner of the *Journal,* Bruce was a shrewd promotor. By 1897 he had built the circulation up to 44,000 copies[14] and sold the Journal to both school board members *and* superintendents. Since he also promoted and helped organize the state association of school boards, Bruce extended further influence when he published lengthy reports of the meetings of these organizations in the *Journal.*[15] He also led the movement for creating a department of school boards within the National Education Association. Such a department was established; it met for the first time in 1896. It is significant that the title of the new organization was not the *Department of School Boards* but the *Department of School Administration.* The drive to establish this department was not unrelated to the attack on school boards made in the Draper Report or to the happenings that took place in Cleveland—Bruce made it clear he was responding to criticism when he made his speech launching the new organization.[16]

Bruce's reaction to the Draper Report was quick and sharp. The Report was given at the end of February, 1895. He responded in March with an editorial entitled "The 'Czar' Movement" in which he accused superintendents of wanting to eliminate school boards. In the April edition Bruce printed a dramatic cartoon along with editorial comments to the Report.[17] The setting for the cartoon was

---

14 He featured some solid articles, he inserted much information which had to be extremely valuable to anyone running a school, and he included numerous news items—at times almost gossip items from all over the country. Finally, and perhaps most important, each issue was filled with photographs of board members and superintendents. Generally a single town such as Webb City, Missouri would be featured. He also printed the latest news regarding the hiring and firing of superintendents, and their salary schedules in many cities.

15 By 1896, four states had organized school board associations. These states were Illinois, Wisconsin, Iowa, and Texas.

16 N.E.A. *Proceedings* (1896), p. 970.

17 The *Journal* regularly carried one large cartoon in its first pages.

the Roman Senate in which all of the characters are dressed in togas. In the foreground is a man lying on the ground with blood flowing from his chest. He is labeled *Vox Populi*. Leaning over this person in a grieving manner is another figure. His label is School Board. In the background, walking away from the scene, are several men with knives in their hands. They are educators. Conspicuous among them is Andrew Draper. In the background under a statue is the inscription "Schools Belong to the People." The title of the cartoon is "Julius Caesar 'Educationalized'." Under the cartoon Bruce reported that the Draper Report "proposes that the School Boards in cities be reduced to a bureau of clerks and the Superintendents elevated to supreme power . . . and, in fact, become the 'Czars' over the American public school system."[18]

In the May edition of the *Journal* Bruce reported, in a column entitled "Educational Tyranny," that he had received "large numbers of letters from all parts of the country" commenting on his attack of the Draper Report. He said the majority of them supported his position opposing the "centralization of power in school affairs." Some of these letters came from city superintendents themselves. He quoted at length from one such letter which ended in these words: "They [the educators] desire the Boards of Education to be mere servants, granting these Boards only one privilege—that of electing these mighty educators to supreme control for life, with the power to employ teachers and run the educational machine without 'let or hindrance.' The people will be exceedingly unwise to let anything out of their hands that deeply concerns them."[19] Those words coming from a prominent superintendent must have pleased school board members and especially their champion, William Bruce.

In the months that followed the main battle, Bruce continued to snipe away at Draper and his associates, accusing them of wanting to eliminate school boards altogether. He charged them with being power-hungry and undemocratic and he warned the country of the dangers involved in centralizing the school system. As part of his strategy, he made frequent attacks on the Cleveland school organization, sometimes attacking its "undemocratic" character and sometimes presenting "evidence" to show that it was a dismal failure. In his dramatic cartoons and in his editorials, he presented Draper and his colleagues as villains. He probably succeeded in making many superintendents feel very guilty.

---

[18] The *Journal*, X, No. 4, p. 1.
[19] The *Journal*, X, No. 5, p. 8.

In his attacks on the Draper Report, in his other frequent statements on the question of the proper role of school boards and
superintendents, and the proper relationship between the two, Bruce
succeeded in muddying the waters. School administrators have
been trying to get them cleared up ever since. He agreed that the
superintendent "should be recognized as the educational expert" but
he was not willing to concede that the boards' function was simply
to legislate, it was also to "administer."[20] When it came down to the
precise duties board members should have, Bruce, in this period at
least, was vague, but it is clear that he intended for them to have
educational duties.[21] The result was that the distinction between the
"legislative" function and the "executive" function was blurred and
apparently, despite decades of effort by school administrators, remains blurred. William Bruce was, of course, not the only person
responsible for this development. But he was the leader. He sent out
questionnaires to school board members asking for their views on
who should have what power and he printed many of their replies in
the *Journal*. He encouraged the discussion of the problem in the state
school board association meetings. How to resolve this problem was
one reason he brought the national organization of school boards
into existence. In their discussions (which Bruce published) leading
board members disagreed and their views ranged (as might have
been expected) from those in favor of having the board hire the
superintendent and letting him run the schools to those who believed
the board should hire teachers, select textbooks, etc. None of them
at any time advocated doing away with school boards. Even the most
liberal took the position that the board should have the final authority—which it did have and still has. As William Mowry said, *"Everyone knows how reluctant men are to give up authority when once
they have secured it, however small or brief it may be."*[22]

At the same time, the battle between superintendents and school
boards was going on in thousands of school districts all over the
country. It was here that the actual "fighting" took place and it was

20 N.E.A. *Proceedings* (1896), pp. 970–973. To get educators on his side, he
argued that if board members were educated about school affairs they would be
more likely to accept the superintendent as an expert.

21 This comes out clearly in his frequent criticism of the move toward having
small boards instead of large ones. In May of 1896, he commented editorially on
the fact that some members of the Chicago school board had resigned because
they did not have the time to do the work. Bruce said that "the labors assigned
to every member of the board are exacting and arduous" and because this was so
he believed that boards should be large, perhaps as large as forty in the largest
cities. Vol. XI, No. 5, p. 3.

22 William A. Mowry, *op. cit.,* p. 40 (Author's italics).

here that there were real "casualties." The question arose: when implementing the recommendation contained in the Draper Report, would there be some casualties among superintendents? Draper's response to this was that there probably would be, but that a superintendent who was not "strong and decided enough to make the position secure is of small consequence to anybody." He urged superintendents to take up the fight—to overcome the "evil-disposed persons and make for righteousness."[23] This was late in February, 1895.

In the months following, many superintendents took Draper seriously and "carried the fight to the enemy." In August, 1895, Bruce gave the following account of the battle. Under the title "Deposing Superintendents," he wrote: "We have observed with interest, *and in some cases with regret,* the fierce contests which have been waged in many school boards this summer over the retention or dismissal of superintendents. So fiercely have some of these contests been waged that the press and the public have been wrought to the highest pitch." He reported that superintendents A. P. Marble of Omaha and P. W. Search of Los Angeles "and others equally prominent" had been fired. He noted that the "decapitation of so high a school official was an unpleasant task wrought with strife and ill-feeling." Then he stated the bald truth about the superintendent's position in American education: *"The superintendent's position is a difficult one. He is the ready target for unreasonable parents, disgruntled teachers and officious school board members. In a vortex of school board quarrels, he is the first to become crushed."*[24]

---

[23] N.E.A. *Proceedings* (1895), p. 397.

[24] *American School Board Journal,* XI, No. 2, pp. 8–9 (Author's italics).
There is abundant evidence that Bruce's description of the job was an accurate one *and* that the situation has not changed. It will be impossible to get the data to tell the story of how much pain and anguish has been caused to superintendents and their families by these struggles which have occurred repeatedly down through the years. The ultimate tragedy in this connection occurred in Marshalltown, Iowa in 1896. C. P. Rogers had been superintendent there since 1874—*twenty-two years* —and he had been praised publicly by the editor of the *Journal of Education,* A. E. Winship, as being one of the best superintendents in the country. Winship had visited the Marshalltown schools and he knew Rogers. He described him as "a most kind and gentle spirit" and as a "progressive educator, devoted even too exclusively to the interests of his schools." But Rogers had antagonized a prominent physician in Marshalltown who finally succeeded after several failures in getting himself elected to the school board in 1895 and then to the presidency of the board in 1896. In July of 1896 he was featured and praised by Bruce in his journal for his active participation in discovering deficiencies in the schools. In January of 1896 Superintendent Rogers resigned. During the summer of 1896 he was unable to find another job. Early in September he committed suicide. *Journal of Education,* XLIV, No. 11 (September 17, 1896), p. 196.

William Bruce's response to this problem was to urge school board members to be more magnanimous in carrying out their "sacred trust." They should never, he said, act out of prejudice or revenge or selfishness.[25] In other words they should behave like gods not men. Incidentally, the solutions to the problem suggested by the leaders in school administration, especially those safe under tenure in universities, have been equally unrealistic. One of their suggestions was to have superintendents be Lincoln-like characters.[26]

Results. In the years that followed, both educators and board members continued to discuss and debate the question of the proper function of superintendents and school board members along with other matters (such as the size of school boards) that had been raised by the Draper Committee. School board members disagreed among themselves on everything but the fact that the school board was the final authority. Educators generally backed the Draper Report and worked to have the superintendent made all-powerful on educational policy within the school. Sometimes they sought to do this by convincing school board members to delegate authority, and, at other times, they sought to achieve power through law as Draper had recommended.

With each year that passed changes were made and these in the direction of implementing most of the recommendations made by the Draper Committee. Schools *were* largely removed from partisan politics. School boards *were* reduced in size. Superintendents *were* reduced in number. Superintendents *were* gradually given the power to hire teachers, and select textbooks, and control the educational program generally. But two of the basic recommendations *were not* put into effect. One was that of separating the business and instructional aspects of the superintendency. After 1910 Superintendent Frank Spaulding of Newton, Massachusetts led the attack against this separation.[27] The other major recommendation not achieved was that of making the superintendent independent. This development became a major factor influencing the nature of the American public school system in the twentieth century.

The fact was—no amount of legal action granting authority to the superintendent or defining his function or the boards' could change

---

25 *Ibid.*

26 *Educational Leadership Progress and Possibilities,* The Eleventh Yearbook of the Department of Superintendence of the N.E.A. (Washington, D.C.: The Association, 1933), p. 159.

27 For details *see* Raymond E. Callahan, *Education and the Cult of Efficiency* (Chicago: University of Chicago Press, 1962), pp. 188–196.

the basic element in the power structure. *So long as the school board retained, as it did, the power of appointment and dismissal of the superintendent he could not be independent.* Furthermore, since board members were elected by citizens in the local districts, the superintendent could not be independent of the community. These factors, plus (1) the inadequate financial arrangements which have produced a situation of chronic financial crisis, and (2) the immense difficulty of educating all the children "to the limit of their abilities" in a massive industrial society have turned the super-intendent's job into what one superintendent, writing anonymously in 1916, described as "the most hazardous job known to insurance actuaries,"[28] and what a prominent layman, writing in 1955, de-scribed as "the most harassing and ulcer producing job in public life."[29]

The failure of superintendents to win "independence" was one outcome of the battle of 1895. The superintendent *has* gained great power *vis-a-vis* the teachers and the children, but he is in a vulner-able position in regard to the school board and the community. The former condition is partly responsible for the present unrest among teachers, and the latter condition has shaped and fashioned the job and the men who have held it. The job has required cautious, con-servative individuals who have the ability to manipulate people.[30] It is men with these qualities who have been "leading" public educa-tion.

Another important outcome of the 1895 encounter was the failure on the part of superintendents to get school board members to accept definite limitations in their role—especially in their role of making educational policy decisions which superintendents believe should be made by educators. William Bruce was the leader in blur-ring the distinction. He helped to build what Willard Waller has called a "tradition of interference" in school affairs on the part of both board members and ordinary citizens.[31]

Partly because of Bruce, the bold effort made by superintendents in 1895 failed. The persons who suffered were the superintendents because, when they failed in their struggle with boards of education, they lost their jobs. Since 1895 the leaders in administration have

---

28 "Why Superintendents Lose Their Jobs," *American School Board Journal,* LII, No. 5 (May, 1916), p. 18.

29 Henry Toy, Jr. in *The School Executive,* January, 1955, p. 98.

30 For an excellent account of how the job had moved in this direction by 1932, *see* Willard Waller's classic work, *The Sociology of Teaching* (New York: John Wiley & Sons, Inc., 1932).

31 Willard Waller, *op. cit.,* p. 94.

spent their energy not in frontal attacks on the system, but rather by working within the given framework and spending much time and energy trying to *educate* and *persuade* school board members as to what their proper role should be. Almost every book published on school administration in the twentieth century has a section on the relationship between school boards and superintendents—what it is and what it should be. In these sections the authors invariably complain about school boards who interfere in the "professional" work of the school, thereby revealing that the "tradition of interference" continues.[32]

Though not gaining total victory in the battle of 1895, superintendents have been making more of the major educational decisions year after year in the twentieth century. They have been in command. But it has been an uneasy command—for they hold this power at the mercy of school boards whom they have had to please, and boards may play the role of educator at their pleasure. In addition their problem is now being complicated from below. The troops are getting restive and in some places there has already been rebellion in the ranks.

Teachers and Policy Control

Teachers have not been involved in the fight to control policy until recently. Formerly, only an occasional voice was raised in their behalf. Professor Albert Bushnell Hart of Harvard had asked the Draper Committee to consider the possibility of giving teachers a voice in running the schools and he actually appeared at the Cleveland meeting in February, 1895, when the Report was submitted, to argue his case. He asked the Committee to arrange the school organization so that teachers would be consulted systematically on a "definite" and "permanent" basis. He suggested that this could be

---

[32] *See* Ellwood P. Cubberley's *Public School Administration* (Boston: Houghton-Mifflin Co., 1916), pp. 110–111 and 118–121. The following statement from the Eleventh Yearbook of the Department of Superintendence (1933), p. 158, is typical:

"Many difficulties reported grow out of the superintendent's relations with his board of education. *The board members frequently seem to usurp the superintendent's function.* This tendency is an *embarrassing* and *delicate* matter for the superintendent. Subcommittee organization of the board frequently results in *officiousness* on the part of *committee members* in *meddling in professional matters.* Board members sometimes use influence in securing appointment of friends and local people regardless of merit. *There is evidence that some members lack an adequate concept of the province of a board member.*" (Author's italics.)

done by establishing teacher's councils.[33] Andrew Draper took the floor to reply to Hart. He was, he said, in favor of consulting teachers—all good superintendents were. But he opposed the idea of creating councils of teachers and giving them legal standing because "the result would be a combination among the teachers—politics of the poorest kind—to coerce the superintendent."[34] In other words, superintendents were having enough trouble with school boards; why complicate their situation by giving teachers any power.

In 1903 John Dewey provided evidence as to the degree of teacher participation there was in policy decisions. He wrote:

> As to the teacher: If there is a single public school system in the United States where there is *official* and *constitutional* provision made for submitting questions of method of discipline in teaching, and the questions of curriculum, textbooks, etc., to the discussion of those actually engaged in the work of teaching, the fact has escaped my notice; indeed, the opposite situation is so common that it seems, as a rule, to be absolutely taken for granted as the normal and final condition of affairs. The number of persons to whom any other course has occurred as desirable, or even possible—to say nothing of necessary—is apparently very limited." [35]

This situation described by Dewey, and especially the lack of any notion of *official and constitutional provision,* has prevailed, with few exceptions, down to the present time. Why should this have been so? There have been several reasons. First, is the fact that the great majority of teachers in America have been women. The teaching "profession" has been a feminine profession. Partly for biological reasons and partly because of the male ego, it has been difficult for men to become full-time professionals or to get professional recognition. Women as teachers have suffered along with "women as women" in being denied certain rights. Most women teachers in the past were young, unmarried and often poorly educated. All these factors have combined in producing the "image" of the teacher (and especially the elementary teacher) as a combination governess and baby sitter. A few items selected from the *American School Board*

---

33 N.E.A. *Proceedings* (1895), p. 393. Some Councils were established and the one in Chicago under Supt. Ella Flagg Young had real power after 1910. However, when William McAndrew became superintendent in the twenties, he fought the Council and reduced its power.

34 *Ibid.,* p. 397.

35 This statement was made in an article published in *The Elementary School Teacher* in December, 1903. The article was reprinted in a collection of Dewey's articles in *Education Today* (New York, 1940), p. 64. (Author's italics.)

Journal give some indication of the status accorded to teachers in the 1890's.

> Lima, O. Board of Education has forbidden the teachers to take any part in politics, except to vote.
>
> The Steubenville, O., board will dismiss teachers who do their buying out of the city.
>
> The school directors of Hopewell Township, Pa., have officially declared against scholars making love to teachers during school hours.
>
> Grand Rapids, Mich. The school board has decided that each school teacher, before signing her contract, must swear that she will entertain no matrimonial propositions during the year.
>
> The Blue Mound, Kas., school board has a peck of trouble on its hands. The teacher objects to making the fire and sweeping out any longer and demands a janitor.

A second factor which has slowed the entrance of teachers into the power struggle has been the very nature and operation of its own major professional association—the National Education Association. This organization has done much good work but, despite its great size since 1920, it has not been able to help teachers gain power. That this should be so is not surprising. First, the organization has suffered from the factors discussed above—the feminine nature and the rather low educational level (until recently) of its members. But an equal hindrance has been the nature of the organization's leadership. After all, there are many men in teaching and they are in the N.E.A. Unfortunately for teachers, the leaders in the N.E.A., and especially in the permanent bureaucracy, have been former school administrators. In addition, the most influential department of this "teachers" organization has been its Department of Superintendence. It is obvious that, while teachers and superintendents have much in common (including their interest in education), they also have areas in which their interests conflict. Thus, it would have been unrealistic to expect the superintendents to push hard for a powerful teachers association which would have forced them to negotiate with it over such matters as salary or teaching load. It has always been much easier for superintendents and for school boards to deal with teachers as individuals.

By 1915 some teachers had become frustrated with the N.E.A., bolted the organization, and formed the American Federation of Teachers. When the new organization gave signs of healthy growth, the administrative leaders, both in the N.E.A. and outside it, fought it in two ways. They appealed to the status-consciousness of teachers by representing the A.F.T. as being "union" and "blue-collar." And they launched a drive to bring all teachers into the N.E.A.[36]

William Bruce helped carry on this drive through numerous cartoons and editorials. The strategy worked. The A.F.T. remained small and, until recently, relatively ineffective. The N.E.A. after 1920 grew quickly to mammoth size but it continued to be dominated by the administrator group.

There was a third factor responsible for the slow progress teachers have made in gaining some voice in determining educational policy. This factor was the conception of school administration which developed and became very strong after 1910. The notion was that there was a parallel between education and industry. The school was seen as a factory or business enterprise which, as an industry, was run by a board of directors. This board, in turn, hired a managerial expert who hired workers and directed production. Translated into education this meant that the expert was the superintendent hired by the school board. He in turn hired the teachers (workers) who worked on the pupils (the product). Since the board and the managerial expert in industry did not give workers a vote in policy-making, why should they in education.[37]

After 1929 there was a strong reaction against this authoritarian conception in educational administration. Under the leadership of Jesse Newlon it was replaced, at the level of ideology at least, by the concept of "democratic administration." John Dewey stated what this concept meant in a speech before the Department of Superintendence in 1937. "The democratic principle requires," he said, "that every teacher should have some regular and organic way in which he can, directly or through representatives democratically chosen, participate in the formation of the controlling aims, methods and materials of the school of which he is a part."[38] The next year the great leader in school administration, George Strayer, endorsed the democratic notion in an important statement made for the Educational Policies Commission of the N.E.A. But Strayer also stated that on any policy *"The final authority must rest with the school*

---

36 For a detailed account of these actions *see* Ralph D. Schmidt, *A Study of the Organizational Structure of the N.E.A. 1884–1921* (Unpublished doctoral thesis, Washington University in St. Louis, 1963). *See* especially Chapter VI.

37 For an analysis of this development *see* Raymond E. Callahan, *Education and the Cult of Efficiency,* especially pp. 79–94 and 148–153.

38 John Dewey, "Democracy and Educational Administration," reprinted in *Education Today,* p. 343.

board."[39] By the late 1930's teachers had arrived at somewhat the same position superintendents had been in after 1895. Practically everyone agreed that they *should* have more of a voice but in the final analysis it was up to the school board and to the superintendent as to whether they would or not. Certainly since 1940, teachers have served on more committees than they had previously, but this author's impression is that teachers in most school districts have the *appearance* but not the *substance* of power.

In the 1960's evidence abounds that teachers have been becoming more and more dissatisfied with their traditional position of being ignored and that they have become more militant in their demands for a voice in determining educational policy.[40] Why should this be so? There are at least two major reasons. First, teachers have changed—they are now educated persons (many with masters degrees from the finest universities) and they are tired of being treated as children. The second reason is that teachers have been influenced by Myron Lieberman. His first book in 1956 and his second in 1962 helped bring the unrest felt among teachers to the level of consciousness.[41] He shattered the illusion that education was a great profession. He pointed out that teachers were probably the weakest occupational group in the country. He told teachers bluntly that if they wanted more professional freedom and more control over educational policy they would have to strengthen their organizations, enter the arena, and fight. Since one of the leaders of the N.E.A. stated publicly that teachers "are in a state of ferment bordering on rebellion," it is clear that the battle is underway.[42]

---

[39] George Strayer, *The Structure and Administration of Education in American Democracy* (Washington, D.C.: Educational Policies Commission of the N.E.A., 1938), pp. 59, 67. (Author's italics.)

[40] I am thinking especially of the actions of the New York City teachers who have won the legal right to bargain with the board and also the actions of the teachers of Utah and Oklahoma.

[41] Myron Lieberman, *Education as a Profession* (Englewood Cliffs, N.J.: Prentice-Hall, Inc., 1956), and *The Future of Public Education* (Chicago: University of Chicago Press, 1962).

[42] Allan M. West, "What's Bugging Teachers?" in *Saturday Review,* October 16, 1965, p. 88.

CHAPTER III

The Social Structure of the Teaching Profession

OSWALD HALL

Department of Sociology, University of Toronto

New Terms—New Developments in Teaching

There are many warnings that all is not well in the world of teaching. The educational system bristles with ominous new terms—conflict, power, power systems, rising power. Educators must focus attention on an easily-neglected aspect of education—the fact that a continuous wrestling match goes on between those who do the work of teaching and those who organize that work.

The new terms bring one face to face with arresting developments in the field of education. By and large people are unprepared for these developments. For many the images of education involve recollections of the little red one-room school house presided over by a single teacher, who managed all the grades, and maintained an unquestioned deference toward the members of the school board. These things have changed: between the teacher and the board there has arisen a veritable army of administrators.

The school systems are very complicated. The school boards, the school administrators, and the powerful teacher organizations are only part of the total system. Another term is needed, one which will describe the teachers in their every-day capacity—some collective term like "the teaching profession," or teaching "corps." A place should be found too for the student in the system—one could argue that he is what the system is all about. A place, too, should be found for the parent, who appears as voter, tax-payer, or sometimes just a bothersome parent.

Some day historians may provide answers to a set of intriguing questions: how did parents and other citizens come to generate the immensely powerful structures called school boards? Why did some teachers desert teaching and turn into administrators? How did individual teachers band together into organizations vast enough to frighten both administrators and board members? Since these questions belong to the historian, the task is that of pulling into view some of the tangled threads that make up the fabric of relationships between school boards and teacher organizations.

Consider three questions: (1) What is the current relationship of teaching to the rest of society? (2) What occupational models are teachers choosing and following? (3) What change can be detected in these two realms of observation, with particular reference to the effects of the changing recruitment patterns in teaching.

To begin with, the terms in this discussion may be ambiguous. Using the word "union" instead of "teacher organization" and "professional associations" could simplify the discussion. In talking about unions and unionization, wouldn't one word take the place of four? Why use the term "profession" to refer to teachers? Why use such an honorific term when it patently does not fit the facts? Misunderstandings arise because the vocabulary is terribly cluttered; pleasant terms insulate people from unpleasant realities.

In discussing the relation of teaching to society, four terms are used to signify the distinctive aspect of the teacher. The terms are "public servant," "parent surrogate," "custodial personnel," and "professional." About each of these terms several things should be said.

Any occupation can be carried on in various ways, and some of these are likely to be more satisfying than others to the people in the occupation. How varied have been the models of teaching in various societies: in Greece, teaching was a task for slaves; in India, a task for highly-respected old men; in Quebec, a task for religious personnel; in Ireland, for "brat-busters"; in much of rural North America, for sweet-faced farmers' daughters, for whom a teacher's certificate was in reality a hunting license to get a husband.

Teaching Today

How is teaching seen in the present day and age? Teachers are viewed in most part as members of the public service, as public servants. This view of the teacher emphasizes the fact that he is an employee. He is hired by a public organization, which pays him a salary and sets up the regulations and rules under which he works.

His daily work is superintended by superintendents, inspected by inspectors, directed by principals, co-ordinated by vice-principals, ruled and regulated by the clock and the almanac, and recorded by registrars in registers. Ostensibly all this is done for the welfare of the student and to the acclaim of his fellow teachers. From this perspective the teacher is first and foremost a part of a vast organizational system. The larger and more complex the system becomes, the more the teacher becomes a cog in that organization. It envelopes him entirely, and there is no escape. When at last he retires, the organization still pursues him with his pension check. The only simple way he can escape its clutches is by a substantial misdemeanor. Therefore, the teacher is first and foremost a bureaucrat, working in a bureaucratic setting.

If, alternatively, attention is focused, not on the bureaucratic system but on the parent, the teacher appears to fill a different role. In American society families turn their children over to the teacher to a greater and greater degree. Schooling has become a matter of urgent concern to parents. Indeed schooling has become one of the few durable benefits a modern parent can bequeath his children. Without education the latter are almost powerless to enter the working world. Parents recognize that the longer the child can remain in school the higher is the life-time price tag that will attach to his services. They realize also that only at school can the child develop special skills and abilities which will enable him to compete favorably with and against his age mates. Because parents themselves can do so little to help their children constantly keep abreast in this world of expanding knowledge, they turn to the teacher to do for their children what is beyond their own competence.

In this perspective the teacher stands revealed as the parent surrogate; he does what the parent cannot do. In such cases, the concern and anxiety of the parent determines the role of the teacher— they become the social mechanisms that generate the pattern of the teacher's place in society. In this light, the teacher is not a cog in a governmental bureaucracy; he is the source of salvation for the child in a world in which the only salvation is well-paid work.

In discussing teaching from the above two perspectives, other facets are ignored. In a very real sense schools are custodial in character, a fact that is not satisfying to teachers. Perhaps teachers have always been, in part, custodial figures, but one tends to ignore this. Perhaps the truancy officer represents the proper custodial figure and the teacher is never seen in that light. On the one hand, it may be that teachers do their work so well that no truancy officers are needed; on the other hand, it may be that the teachers have actually become the custodial figures that truancy officers once were.

At any rate, this feature of teaching has vastly increased in recent years. For one thing, children are more and more restricted to a school style of life. Few children can have jobs outside school. Few can ever see their parents at work. Few can get into a work place until they are adults. It is as though there were a great conspiracy to keep children away from the world of work. Child labor laws prevent it. Walls and fences are built around work places. For the child the only legitimate place to be is in the school. In addition, the time the youngster spends in school has been immensely lengthened. All youngsters are expected to stay in school until they are the size of adults. In some cases they are kept there until long after they have earned the right to vote.

Maintaining custody of youngsters becomes more and more complicated and more and more difficult as adults are increasingly added to pupil population and at the same time everybody is kept in the school longer. When the child no longer has a choice as to whether or not he goes to school, then the school has to accept and be responsible for even the most unruly and unpromising types of youngsters. This heightens the custodial aspect of teaching.

To say that teaching is, in some part, a custodial function is to place teachers among the other great custodial occupations of society. Here teachers link hands with nurses who take charge of patients confined to a hospital, and with jailers, the reform school personnel, the army sergeants, the penitentiary guards, the baby-sitters, and all those whose occupation is to maintain control of people put in their charge. One learns a great deal about teachers and about schools by associating them with those occupations with which they have much in common.

Perhaps this analysis pushes the teaching occupation along a path which it never sought, but this is common-place in society. Most occupations become involved in performing functions which they never envisioned at the outset.

Professional perspective.   It clarifies what is meant here by the term "profession" if it is preceded by the adjective "independent." From this perspective the teacher is an autonomous worker, one who creates the appropriate conditions for his own work. He creates in his work rather than having it created for him. He decides what is good for his clients; he chooses what should go into the curriculum; he decides how his students should be evaluated; he determines how they should behave toward him; he selects new recruits for his work; he determines the character of their training; he sits in judgment on his colleagues; he specifies his own conditions of work.

The model of an independent profession is probably the most attractive work model found in our society. It is the one called to mind by the practice of medicine. Law and the priesthood have much the same sort of pattern. Traditionally, these occupations have occupied a high status and have been accorded prestige. They stand above society in a sense; by the same token their clients stand far below them on the social scene. Professionals set their own standards; in this sense, they are "free and independent." If the professional worker is accountable to anyone in society, it is to one of his own colleagues.

Following the model of an independent profession, teaching should be done by those who work at the command or demand of their customers or clients. It should be performed by workers who put themselves in the position of deciding what should be done for their customers or clients. Since teaching can be organized in large scale fashion in such a way that bureaucratic officials decide what is good for both worker and customer (that is, for teacher and student), teaching loses its status as an independent profession.

Teacher aspiration and realities.   Teachers do tend to view themselves as members of an independent profession. They aspire to a high level of deference and respect. They aspire to make consequential decisions regarding education. They like to think that they should be allowed to determine curricula. They view themselves as being the best judges of who should be recruited into teaching, and how these recruits should be trained. They would like to help decide the size of their own pay checks.

Of course, the actualities are quite otherwise. Teachers are hired by big employers. School boards and state departments make the major decisions about their work. Government agencies prescribe their training and decide who shall be recruited. Outside agencies take the initiative in trying to get teachers to improve the quality of their work and to raise the level of their qualifications. Boards and government departments prescribe the curricula of their daily lives; they supervise, inspect, and evaluate the product of the teacher's work. No matter how bravely teachers may wish for the status of the "independent profession," they are anchored firmly (though not irrevocably) in the status of service employees.

Union organization among teachers, therefore, does not stem from an emerging professionalization. The current vigorous forms of association of teacher groups have emerged at a time when there is extremely little professional orientation in evidence. The explanation for strong union organization must be sought along other lines.

The nature of the enterprise.   In considering the kinds of occupational models available to teachers within a given framework, that of the large scale corporate school system, various alternative daily work models are available. Three are selected. Again the terms used may sound unfamiliar: "good employees," "men with a calling" and "racketeers."

If teachers are fundamentally employees in urban society, it is useful to raise questions about distinctive kinds of employees. To consider what a *"good"* employee is, he is one who is responsive to rules. He gives a fair day's work for a fair day's pay. He grants deference to his superiors. He avoids tyrannizing his subordinates. He learns the rules of the game and tries to fit into the expectations of the school he is in. He neither embarrasses his colleagues by acting the "eager beaver," nor alienates them by skimping on his work. Such employees are the salt of the earth. If all were like him, administration would take care of itself automatically.

In any school system one is likely to find teachers who go far beyond the requirements of a good employee. Some are whole-heartedly devoted to their work. They live "for" their work rather than living "off" it. Some of them could not envisage themselves in any other sort of work. These are the people who belong irrevocably to the occupation they are in. In a real sense they have experienced a "calling" and their work is both their vocation and their avocation. They are men with a "mission" in their lives. However, their presence does not necessarily make life easier for the administrator. Sometimes such devotion may be downright painful for the administrator who likes a "happy ship."

To understand the nature of a "calling" in the work world is to delve deeply into the human being. It may be that such a man has taken a vow which planted a permanent compass in his inner self. It may be that a compelling sense of faithfulness to his life work permeates him from day to day. To explore these matters fully would involve psychology and that is not the task here.

Workers with a "calling" contrast with workers who deviate from the norm to the opposite direction. For some workers the abiding concern is not what they put into their work but what they draw out. If work is thought of as a symmetrical system of rights and duties, they presumably tend to skimp the duties and maximize the rights. They may go even further and embroider a set of privileges to add to their rights. They often press for shorter hours and lightened work load, for escape from special duties, for relief time in which others carry on for them, for a higher level of remuneration, for fringe benefits (such as parking space, staff recreation rooms, meal service), for increased vacations, and so forth. In corresponding fashion, they may reduce their duties to a purely nominal level. When duties reach the vanishing point and rights and privileges are maximized, the "racket" exists. In all occupations there are racketeers of sorts as well as men with a "calling." Somewhere between these extremes, the category of the "good" employee is established.

"Labels" on teachers.   Different kinds of teachers can be documented readily by noting the labels teachers apply to themselves. One currently recognized category is the "trousseau" teacher. For the girl whose parents cannot provide a dowry for her and who, herself, cannot find a husband able to support her immediately, teaching is a single solution to a dual problem inasmuch as it actually permits her time to accumulate a dowry while she is on the prowl for a husband. Another term, "Buick" teacher, designates a second type—the boy for whom teaching represents a quicker route to highly-valued consumer goods than any other readily available. There are other favorite "labels" for teachers.

One finds a set of terms which aptly describe the recognized variants in every well-developed occupation. Some of these spring from the various ways the occupation can be practiced. Some of the labels of an earlier era of teaching are mostly forgotten. Once the terms "progressive education" and "progressive teachers" were popular. Presumably there were labels for the not so progressive, including reactionary. Today there are teachers who welcome change and champion it; there are others who prefer comfortable well-worn ruts. Reality persists, though the names may change.

The nature of the practice.   To consider the third main segment—trends of change in the field of education—some trends are taken for granted and thus escape the attention. Nevertheless, they cast light on the current liveliness and power of teachers' organizations. The main concern here is: what are the consequences of recruiting varied sorts of people into teaching?

To begin with a general observation, teaching is not one occupation, but two. There are men teachers and women teachers. On this continent at the level of higher education (college and university), the work is overwhelmingly men's work. At the level of primary education it is equally restricted to women. At the secondary school level an ambiguous situation exists, one where both men and women function. It is relevant to ask whether the occupation itself, at the high-school level, is viewed as masculine or feminine. It is readily recognized that some women teachers are decidedly masculine, just as some men teachers may be equally feminine. What is really consequential is whether the occupation itself is viewed as masculine or feminine. Do high-school students view it as feminine? How is it viewed in the larger society?

The existence of large numbers of women in teaching in America has important consequences for the teaching occupation, though not for the reasons usually assumed. Women have had an unmistakable impact on the teaching occupation, not because they are feminine, but rather because of the distinctive career orientation they have brought into the work.

Teaching—a job or career.   There are two distinct ways in which a person can approach an occupation—one may treat it as a job, or treat it as a career. Women treat teaching as a job. (It can be a very pleasant job—offering a five-hour day, a five-day week, and a three months' holiday). In labeling teaching a "job," several things are implied. Women prefer that it be easy to enter, rather than difficult to get into. Ideally, one merely shows a certificate and one is hired. They prefer also that it be easy to leave. One need not commit herself to teaching for more than a year at a time. As a supply teacher, she need commit herself to work only for a day at a time. Women prefer that it be easy both to leave and to re-enter. One can desert the field for years, and re-enter it merely by dusting off a certificate. Apparently to them teaching skills do not deteriorate through disuse. Women also prefer that there be a uniform salary scale. One begins her teaching almost immediately at full salary scale; one can absent herself from the field for a decade and return at the level of the salary scale. In other words, she prefers to move from place to place, from job to job, and be assured of the same sort of salary scale.

The organization of school systems reflects these interests of its women members. Hence there is little of a career in teaching. There is no recognized path to excellence. There is no accepted procedure by which one becomes a "master" teacher or a "star" in the field. There is no sequence of progressively demanding stages to which one can aspire. There is no recognition, public or monetary, no hard-won technical expertise. Teachers resent and reject, almost unanimously, the notion of "merit" payment. By implication all teachers work at a homogeneous, undifferentiated level.

If one wishes a career in teaching, he must get out of teaching. The usual road out of teaching is into administrative school work or even into administration of teachers' associations. Here one can have a genuine career. One can administer a small unit, and, if he feels his talents are not adequately utilized, he can try his abilities in a larger, more complex, sphere. If a principal feels he has acquired adequate expertise, he can try to superintend the schools of a local system. From there he can go on to larger municipal systems or state systems. In other words, he can enter a work system in which there is a graded series of challenging work situations; here are established ways of recognizing the merit of his services at any level. In school administration one "goes somewhere." This is essentially what is involved in a career.

The woman teacher's approach.   Women teachers apparently do not see teaching as a career. They seem to view teaching as an adjunct to their domestic lives. They want it to be something they can slip into, and step out of, as it suits their interests in their homes and/or families. They don't wish to be penalized by reduced incomes as a result of such "in and out" membership in the occupation. They want to be able to follow their families from city to city and to step into a teaching job in each new location.

Of all feminine occupations, teaching seems to fit most neatly the demands of domestic life: the hours are short and extremely regular; there is no shift work and no night work as in nursing. Travel complications are few. One can leave home after the morning household rush is over, and return before the evening rush begins. The holidays are numerous and fit well into the family's yearly round of life.

Moreover, this orientation of women to teaching is firmly accepted by school boards. They set the rules making it convenient for the teacher to treat her occupation as a mobile, short-term job. They organize the schools in such a manner that there is practically no way a person can achieve a career therein. If a man ambitious for a career comes along, he is effectively precluded from achieving one as a teacher. He uses the teaching occupation as a stepping stone into administration. But there is no door in teaching itself which opens the way to a career.

It is precisely the nature of professions that they *do* offer the opportunity for a career. One can start at a lowly level, gradually achieve greater expertise, develop a reputation, and climb to great heights of recognition and reward. In many fields of work, such as medicine and law, the work is organized in such a way as to facilitate both the possibility of a career and the sense of a career.

But this is not true in school teaching. Here the chance for career is blocked by the current orientation of the teachers and the organizing procedures of the school boards. Both of these things stand foursquare to prevent teaching from becoming a career and/or a profession. Of course, if a career were possible in teaching, it still would not follow automatically that teaching would become a profession. But where there is no career line available, the work cannot take on a professional pattern.

To repeat, teacher organizations and teachers unions are not products of professionalization. They are emerging in a situation where the occupation is notably non-professional, a situation in which the possibilities of career development are almost completely absent.

From what has been said it might be assumed that whatever is wrong in the world of teaching could be readily righted by bringing in more men teachers. But before adopting facile conclusions, consider some dimensions of the masculine aspect of the field.

The career line approach.   It has already been noted that, although there is no career available in teaching itself, it is possible to have a career by stepping from teaching into the shoes of a vice-principal or of a principal and turning to the field of administration. This is precisely what has occurred among many men who have entered the teaching field. In this sense, school administrators are refugees and fugitives from the field of teaching. One may query as to why they have turned fugitive? One might assume that they found teaching unattractive and therefore sought this escape route into a more attractive kind of work. Or perhaps they had their eyes on administration all the while and merely endured the ordeals of their courses in teacher training and their baptism on the firing line of the classroom as the price of admission into the world of school administration.

In today's society administration is a highly-prized way of life. It is also one of the most highly masculine fields of work. The men who run organizations in society are recognized as a superior breed, and are well rewarded financially and are accorded a high level of prestige in the world. They are looked on as being big and tough. The world of administrators is the world of successful men. Those who are willing to compete in this world of administration are assured of access to the big rewards of money and of prestige. By contrast, the world of teaching is relatively flat and undistinguished.

Yet there are some very peculiar characteristics to school administration. It is very noticeable that there is little competition in the world of school administration. Not many school principals step outside of education to take a try at administration in other forms of business or industry. They differ in this from other kinds of administrators who seem to love the struggle and competition with new opponents in new kinds of work. School administrators stay close to their own reservations. Moreover, they do not take kindly to competitors entering their world from the outside. Like teachers, they rejoice in the closed shop. Only those wearing the badge of a teacher's certificate get a chance to compete in the world of school administration. There is no pattern of introducing new blood into educational administration from other fields as a way of injecting innovation and enterprise and imaginative experimentation into the field.

Furthermore, the sort of organization a school administrator runs has its distinctive peculiarities. Although run by men, it is largely staffed by women. The administrator sits in a position of power, but he controls a relatively docile staff. School administrators closely resemble the people who run libraries and social work agencies. In each case the administrator, a man, runs an organization made up largely of women. This sort of administrative set-up is vastly different from the usual model of the work world, where men in positions of power have to contend with other men. In some ways, the school principal resembles, not so much the administrator in the world of business and industry, as the patriarch presiding over a harem. The duties differ but the structure is similar.

From all these counts one can say that school administrators have created a sheltered preserve in which to practice the arts of administration. They have created a set of closed posts, entered through a single door. The door is firmly closed against newcomers who might bring a different training or orientation. School administrators refrain from entering into competition with administrators in other fields, an experience that might open their eyes to the self-imposed limits on their thinking and their practices. School board members may do well to pause and ask themselves just what sorts of union organizations are most likely to arise in the situation where, not only do the teachers believe in and practice an immense closed shop, but the administrators (who rule their affairs), have contrived an almost equally extensive type of closed shop for their own lives.

Not all the men who enter teaching have the itch to become administrators. Indeed there seems to be evidence in the recent past that a new type of man is entering school teaching. The higher salaries offered teachers have brought to teaching a different level of the population. The newcomers seem to be drawn from a lower layer of the total class system than was previously the case. Fewer of them are of the scholarly type likely to become men with a "mission" in teaching. Nor are they men who are looking for a back door into administration. More of them are seeing teaching, with its new income scales, as a fast road to an acceptably high salary level.

While they are scarcely likely to have the urge for administrative careers, on the other hand, these newer recruits are very likely to see union organization as a device for getting ahead. Many of them come from a social class and from homes in which union organization is taken for granted, so they are likely to accept it quite readily in the teaching field. Their attitudes toward union organization are likely to be much more aggressive than those of women teachers who, in the past, have tended to feel that union activities were a bit crude for well-behaved, lady-like teachers.

Changes are also taking place in the kinds of women entering the teaching field. The age level has gone up. Fewer of them are young people idealistically hoping to contribute vigorously to the work of the school. More of them have relatively heavy domestic responsibilities. Fewer of them feel a life-time commitment to scholastic and intellectual matters. More of them have settled into middle-aged monotony. Fewer of them feel that teaching is a highly-refined style of life. More of them feel that union organization is part of daily life. The changes in the kinds of men and women coming into teaching may be relatively small. But small changes can trigger very large consequences.

Summary

A number of propositions can be made about the relation of the social structure of teaching to teacher organization.

1. There is very little of a professional character to school teaching. If, by profession, three things are meant—that teachers are highly dedicated in a selfless fashion to their work; that they have achieved a high level of knowledge and expertise; and that they are prepared to make important decisions about the organization and control of their work, then teaching ranks low on any professional scale.

2. Teaching has become highly feminized and highly domesticated. For many teachers their work is a secondary concern in their lives. Their first and main concerns have to do with family and household responsibilities. Teaching is mainly a source of a paycheck to spread over these other responsibilities.

3. Men who have come into teaching have tended to leave it early in favor of administrative careers. Teaching for them does not represent a life-time commitment to the work into which they have stepped. Teaching is a stepping stone to administration. It is a stepping stone of a peculiar sort—a stepping stone into the back door of the world of administration.

4. School boards have contrived a school system manned by teachers of the above orientations and administered by a distinctive type. They have faced serious hazards in contriving such school systems, and they have done their share in perpetuating the conditions in which teachers and administrators of the above sorts thrive. They have done little to generate new types of teachers or of school administrators.

5. Large scale school organizations provide a favorable environment for large scale mass organizations of teachers. The very size of the units provides a challenge to union organizers. There is enough money in teachers' pockets nowadays to facilitate teacher organization. For the union leaders there is the sense of heady success in creating large, and in some cases opulent, organizations where none existed previously. The omens for their continued growth and power look very favorable.

Disquietudes

Are there developments of a different sort on the horizon? Are there ways of intervening in the present struggles in teacher-board relations—in the recurrent strategies of attack and counter-attack?

These struggles readily become classic examples of vicious circles, where each step plunges the pair deeper into conflict. It may be, however, that the vicious circles can become "beneficent" circles if the antagonists try to look outward a bit more. If they do look outward, they may sense the vague disquietudes in the world of teaching that are obscured today by the power struggles going on between teacher organizations and school boards.

What are these disquietudes? There is a feeling that the schools are not reaching the disadvantaged lower class child in American cities. There is a sense of frustration that if such children are not reached early, they are condemned to a useless march through the years of the school system. There is fear that the body of knowledge is growing so large that the school curriculum does not fully introduce the student to this world of knowledge. There is an uneasiness that science deserves a greater place in schools than has ever been granted. There is a parallel anxiety that mathematics belongs much closer to the heart of education than teachers have been ready to concede. There is an additional fear that schools are failing dismally to prepare students for the work world of tomorrow.

These dark regions of education could come into clearer focus if teachers and school boards would turn away from their current selfish conflicts and level their gaze at these approaching challenges. Each would be discharging its obligations to society much more effectively if the energy of conflict were wisely directed toward problem-solving.

CHAPTER IV

The Future of State Politics of Education

LAURENCE IANNACCONE

School of Education, Claremont University

American education is on the eve of a revolution, first in the state politics and, secondly, in the governing of education in a majority of the states. The impact of several recent decisions by organs of the federal government upon the present general pattern of public school politics, particularly with regard to state legislation, allows it to be predicted that, by the end of the next decade, changes, of a magnitude such as education has not heretofore seen in this century, will take place in the governing of American schools.

Two states are now experiencing the beginning of such changes which might be called a revolution on a small scale. These states are California and Michigan. They provide a basis for comparison with New York State specifically and with the present pattern of state school politics generally. With the factors of change in these two states serving as guide posts, specific hypotheses can be offered concerning the changes in state school politics which lie immediately ahead; however, it is more difficult to assess the long range impact of these events upon teacher groups.

One way to assess the problem of the political power of teacher groups, as it has been influenced by national and state governmental decisions, is to propose a theoretical framework and some hypotheses generated by this, which seem likely to be useful in attacking the problem. The basis for such theory lies in making a comparative analyses of two types of states. One type presents a picture of a general pattern seemingly characteristic of a majority of the states and especially New York. The other type presents a picture of what has happened in some states as the result of the impact of major political changes. The dominant pattern is similar to New York. California and Michigan provide instances of this second category. The major political changes in these states resemble those about to take place in New York (and a number of other

49

states) although they are smaller here than those imminent in New York. The changes in New York's state government probably will have a more rapid and a greater impact upon this state's educational politics than what was observed and is still developing in Michigan and California.

The Prevailing Pattern[1]

The New York State model (with variations) now exists in a majority of eleven states studied recently including New York, New Jersey, Missouri, Maine, Rhode Island, Illinois, and Connecticut. It existed in Michigan before Soapy Williams' election and in California before Governor Brown's election. This basic pattern may be described in a number of ways depending upon the concepts one chooses to use. Recent research in this area focused upon the activities of schoolmen and their friends with regard to legislation. Whichever concepts are used, it is most useful to confine oneself to the legislative realm. Here the prevailing pattern, with regard to legislation specifically, will be described in terms of: (1) its organizational structures, (2) the dynamics of influencing legislation, (in particular the marshalling of information and the mobilization of grass roots influence), (3) the political myths characteristically used, and (4) the social exchanges which occur between the legislature and the schoolmen's system as well as the changes among the participants within this latter system.

From the point of view of organizational structures, one must consider how state organizations involved in education relate to one another and to the legislature common among these states and realize that there is in existence a schoolmen's pyramid of statewide organizations. In Missouri, the office of Everett E. Keith, the executive secretary of the Missouri State Teachers Association, is such an apex. New Jersey's centers in the "Princeton Group" with the New Jersey Education Association, the state department, and the school board association. According to the reports of the Syracuse team and Michael Usdan, New York's apex is in the Educational Conference Board. Before the transitional period—1954 through 1959—California's structure was organized around the Classroom Teachers

[1] See Stephen Bailey et al., Schoolmen in Politics (New York: Institute of Administrative Research, Teachers College, 1963); Michael Usdan, The Political Power of Education in New York State (Syracuse: Syracuse University Press, 1962) and Nicholas A. Masters, State Politics and the Public Schools (New York: Alfred A. Knopf, 1964).

Association. In each case, the National Education Association's state affiliated teachers association occupies a central position through its executive secretary's office. A more detailed examination of these state teacher associations indicates that school administrators play a significant leadership role in them. If one takes the American Federation of Teachers view, which is somewhat outmoded by events in many states such as California, Utah, Oklahoma and Michigan, then one finds they are administrator dominated. The N.E.A. view, however, says that administrator membership is a necessary but not a dominant element. This writer's view differs from both views: historically these state associations have been dominated, indeed, were largely built by school administrators, but more recently bureaucratic developments have taken place in many of these associations with the result that much power now is in the hands of the association career officials. Two hypotheses are suggested for consideration about the prevailing pattern:

> 1. If, historically, these associations were administrator built, then the bulk of those occupying top staff offices (those other than elected ones) were school administrators before they became association careerists.
> 2. If this first hypothesis is borne out, then it seems warranted to infer that the attitudes and values of such careerists, with regard to legislation and legislative programs, will more closely approximate those of school administrators than they do those of teachers.

Were these hypotheses supported by the data, one would have to entertain some doubt as to whether even the state teachers association does, in fact, represent the teachers in its dealings with the legislature—unless one were to argue, paternalistically, that teachers do not know what is good for them, or were to argue that association careerists display the godlike quality of ignoring their own values in the interests of the membership. Even if one were to accept the N.E.A. picture and treat administrators as no more than an essential element in the state teachers association, an examination of the educational apex, and lobby, which takes in the rest of the organizations represented, quickly reveals the nature of the combination involved and the weight one can assign to teacher power.

Typically the "united front" presented by schoolmen and their friends gives one "chair at the table" to the state teachers association; one to the state school boards association; one, or sometimes more, to citizens groups, such as P.T.A. or a big city's association not controlled by teachers; and one or more to associations of school administrators.

The New York State Educational Conference Board is offered as an example of one of the *more open* systems in which pyramiding the organizations of schoolmen and their friends influences legislation. This provides a useful base on which to model the description of the prevailing state pattern. It has served historically as the model for other states. The extent to which the Conference Board has formalized the apex of the pyramid clarifies its components. They are related to one another and to the legislature. The case in Missouri is an example. Also, there is more research available on the New York Conference Board than on the apex of similar educationalist pyramids in other states.[2] This board or "table" has nine "chairs" around it. Four of these belong to school administrator organizations to which teachers may not belong. The fifth seat is occupied by the New York State Teachers Association. (Perhaps enough has been said already about the relationship between teachers and administrators and their influence within the typical state association. The hope is that New York State teacher interests do occupy enough of that seat which they share with administrators so as not to produce too much discomfort at the bottom.) Chair number six is owned by the state School Boards Association.[3] (One notes that when California's pattern was closest to New York's, the school board association's chief advisors on legislation were Edgar Morphet and Hollis Allen, both professors of educational administration. More significantly perhaps, until its old power structure was upset in the mid-fifties, is the fact that its executive secretary was a former school administrator.)

The title deed to the seventh seat at the Conference Board is assigned to the P.T.A. It would be a rash statement indeed to argue that the P.T.A. operates independently of school administrators. Chair number eight is occupied by the New York Citizens Committee for the Public Schools. (Usdan, one judges from his writings, is committed to the virtues of the politically active school administrator and to the New York State model. To the author, Usdan seems carried away when he states, "The Committee's general membership represents an outstanding geographic and vocational cross-

---

[2] Except for Illinois which differs significantly from the prevailing pattern at the point of structural linkage with the legislature.

[3] Details on this association were not reported by either Bailey, *et al.*, or by Usdan. Cooptation at grassroots is, however, cited by Usdan, *op. cit.*, pp. 48, 53, 55, 57, 60.

section of New York State's lay citizenry."[4] Realizing that the citizen's committee consisted of two hundred members in all, one might be permitted a lifted eyebrow at this statement. How many truckdrivers, Negro civil servants, practical nurses and unemployed appear in this "vocational cross-section"? As for geographic representation, Usdan specifically points out that its membership is deliberately gerrymandered against the urban centers.)

The Public School Association of New York City possesses the ninth chair. Without research to help illuminate the detailed political process going on inside the characteristic educational pyramid of schoolmen and their allies, it is not possible to offer a valid judgment on the extent to which New York City teachers are here represented. However, one is well aware that the legal bargaining agent of the teachers of this state's largest school district occupies no seat at this board. In any case, only part of one chair, the New York State Teachers Association's, belongs to teachers.

Much of what has been suggested here may be inferential. Much research needs to be done before one can actually accept or reject the hypotheses offered. Yet one may be wise to consider the conclusions made by the Bailey team: "In reality . . . the Conference Board is a sounding board for and a refiner of the deliberations of an inner core of seven schoolmen."[5]

In most states the list of organizations linked into the monolith characteristic of state educational politics includes one organization not officially represented on the Conference Board. This additional unit (which is characteristically present in the old California pattern; in Missouri's present pattern; in New Jersey, formally; and in New York, informally) is the State Department of Education.

An interlocking directorate supported partly by coopted organizations is evident in New Jersey's apex, the "Princeton Group." Bailey's volume describes the Group:

> . . . these people have worked together a long time. For example, all the departmental officials in attendance had been members of the New Jersey Education Association working committees when they were teachers, and still work with New Jersey Education Association committees as state officials.[6]

In connection with New York State, both Bailey's team and Usdan's writings provide similar evidence. Two of the Conference

---

[4] Usdan, *op. cit.,* p. 24.
[5] Bailey, *et al., op. cit.,* p. 36.
[6] *Ibid.,* p. 38.

Boards "inner core" of seven were state department members.[7] Usdan's report documents (as evidence of the political acumen of schoolmen) how difficult it was even for participants to draw a distinction between those who were staff members of the Conference Board and those who were members of the state department. The commissioner had to write a letter clearing it up.[8]

The first stage of activity.   The early stage of the pyramid's activities was largely one of formulating a legislative program. In New York's case, this involved the work of Paul Mort and the other experts on finance. The Bailey team called the leadership role the "scribbler." Certain information is brought to the Conference Board's discussion and then support is mobilized within the pyramid to demand a Conference Board decision on the annual program. The scribbler's role is particularly significant when a general overhaul of a mandate is in the making. States vary, however, on the number of scribblers available within their boundaries. While New York has not generally turned to experts outside the state for consultant resources on the development of a long-range educational program, other states frequently have done this. One reason the prevailing pattern is so similar in many states is that the number of those scribblers who have played a significant role in influencing master plans in many states is rather small. The Bailey report indicates how Mort and his "principal companion figure," Alfred I. Simpson, left their imprint upon New England, New York, and New Jersey, especially with respect to state educational finance patterns and legislation.[9] In the mid-forties Simpson working with Strayer, Mort's teacher, helped in producing a survey for California which resulted in California's equalization laws. In a similar fashion, it was Edgar Morphet of Berkeley and Lyle Johns of Florida, sometime occupants of graduate student desks in the same room with Mort at Columbia University and at Strayer's feet also, who with Theodore Reller, also of Berkeley, supplied the expertise for the Missouri Citizen's Committee producing this state's mandate in the early fifties. Professors of educational administration in each of these states subsequently supplied a continuing source of expertise and ideas applying the mandate and adapting it over time. Hollis Allen of Claremont University was one of these who left his imprint upon reorganization legislation particularly. The "research findings"

[7] *Ibid.,* p. 36.
[8] Usdan, *op. cit.,* p. 37.
[9] Bailey, *et al., op. cit.,* p. 25.

cited in the Missouri report are almost without exception doctoral dissertations conducted at the University of Missouri in its department of educational administration. In effect, a small interpersonal network of experts, many of whom were trained together, or by one another, provided and continues to provide the "brain trust" for the big ideas which appear as survey reports for given states; then by stages and in pieces these become the pedagogical pyramid's legislative program.

Stage two. The middle stage of the pyramid's activities begins with the adoption of a legislative program and the injection of that program into the legislative process. This stage, however, is chiefly characterized by activities which take the form of marshalling information for legislative committees. This "makes a case" for the proposed legislation. At this point, the role of the research divisions of the pyramid's member organizations and the state department is central to the activities. However united the front, the research groups generally apply their information to the legislative process *separately*. Thus the committee on education, most frequently of the lower house, may be given separate information bearing upon the same proposed legislation. That information, which would appear to come from independent sources of data, reaches the same conclusions. Implicit is the effort to influence the decisions of legislative committees by the pyramid through its research elements. Also evident is the existence of a virtual monopoly of educational information. However many mouths are used, the pyramid speaks with but one voice. The phrase, "monopoly of information," does not suggest that the pyramid deliberately seeks to keep all informational sources to the legislature subservient to its purposes. Instead it is "built in" automatically as an inevitable product of a monolithic structure by the most knowledgeable professionals, interlocking with the state education department.

The third stage. It is the third stage of activities which carries the greatest implications for the impending political revolution. This stage is chiefly characterized by the mobilization of political power at the grass roots, especially in rural legislative districts, and is increasingly significant as a bill moves through its final committee stages and on to the legislature's floors. Here the California Teachers Association capitalized for years upon its relationship with a few key legislators on education and finance committees as well as upon the historic non-partisan leadership of the California legislature, which partly depended for its existence upon the rural edge in representation. In Missouri, similarly, the Missouri State Teachers Association has depended upon its partnership with rural legislators almost entirely. The four case studies of counties briefly reported by Usdan for his description of the mobilization of influence upon legislators in New York are significantly all rural or recently suburban counties.[10] It can be hypothesized that the Missouri State Teachers Association, the California Teachers Association, and the New York State Teachers Association have been effective largely because of their own strong rural structure and representation, which ties well into the heavily unbalanced legislatures favoring rural representation. Two factors help make the rural linkages between the pedagogical pyramids and their legislatures vital in the prevailing pattern. One is the seniority system which adds to the power of the rural areas in contrast to urban ones. Another is that legislators from these districts tend to be more subject to pressure exerted by educational administrators than do those representing large urban constituencies. A truism of educational administration is that the school tends to be the largest business in small town America. It can be hypothesized that the status of school administrators relative to their legislative representatives is higher in those districts which have the greatest chance of profiting most from the seniority system.

The reliance of the schoolmen's pyramids upon rural linkages to help mobilize and influence legislators becomes very clear during the late stages of the legislative process. In Missouri the intermediate office of county superintendent, having no other vital functions in governing education, does function as the relay point for mobilizing school administrators at the county level. St. Louis and Kansas City are passed over in silence. Usdan, significantly, did not cite urban activities of the New York state pyramid. It seems unlikely that in a state such as New York, he would have ignored this if the pyramid placed heavy reliance upon urban legislative links.

The myth.   The power of political myths lies in belief—regardless of the extent to which they reflect fact accurately—although it may be harder to gain acceptance of or maintain political myths which are contrary to fact. The myth of being above political party, as George Washington was reported to be, may be accurate or not but it produced its own halo. A similar char-

---

10 Usdan, *op. cit.,* pp. 44–64.

acteristic is seen in the typical schoolmen's pyramid in New York State; that is, schoolmen project an image clothed in the sacred values characteristic of rural America. Such an image is much easier to maintain where party lines tend to blur inside the legislature. Where party discipline is strong and partisan lines are sharp, the non-partisan finds it harder to get his program through. It was precisely the increased strength of partisanship in Michigan and California which decreased the effectiveness of this same element in their pyramid's myth. Moreover, California's increased party discipline within the legislature's lower house reduced the independence of individual legislators who were strategically placed on Education and Rules and Finance committees. They became more dependent on the political leader. At the same time, the long established ties between C.T.A. and rural Republican assemblymen became more visible. Accurately or not, this tended to be interpreted by some of the Democratic legislators as a covert partisanship. Viewed as covert and therefore dishonest, it was resented by them even more than an open partisanship might have been.

Other changes.   Two other factors added to the shift of representation by rural Republicans to urban Democrats in the lower houses of both California and Michigan. These seem to have impaired seriously a second element in the political myth used by the C.T.A. and M.E.A. One factor involved the A.F.T. gaining a hearing with the legislatures by virtue of their labor allies. The second factor is the increased "bread and butter efforts" made by both the M.E.A. and the C.T.A. at the state legislative level. While it is unlikely that shifts in the legislative power structures produced this increased concern for teacher welfare legislation, an immediate effect of this development was to increase the social distance between the state teacher and state school board associations. It may be hypothesized that this break coupled with the voice of the A.F.T. heard by urban legislators resulted in partially destroying the belief legislators held: that the association, while representing teachers, was primarily concerned with the quality of education. This view was replaced, again, with a more secular view held by the C.T.A.: that the association represented administrators more than teachers and was concerned with membership goals rather than with quality in education. In fact, because of this, C.T.A. headquarters has on occasion asked its administrator association allies to refrain from open support of certain C.T.A. legislative proposals as a kiss of death. Therefore, it may be hypothesized that no single component of the Conference Board can alone project an unselfish image. The sacred community image of being non-partisan, and unselfishly united for the good of school, was the composite political image of schoolmen. This was replaced by a secular image the end of the last decade in California and even earlier in Michigan. The sacred image, as long as it held, constituted a critical element in the effectiveness of the schoolmen's pyramid. The key events leading up to the collapse of this political myth entailed a realignment of political forces inside the states. In California this realignment proceeded as urban Democrats replaced rural Republicans in the control of the lower house.

A fourth way in which the pedagogical pyramid may be seen, as it exists in New York, is in social exchange. The pyramid, particularly its apex, provides useful services to the legislature. It, in turn, serves the pyramid. It may also be deducted that the administrator organizations provide service valuable to the other organizational partners in the pyramid, and so receive a power edge within the pyramid in exchange.

The monolithic system, particularly at its apex, provides the legislatures and individual legislators with expertise. Keith's office in Missouri even writes letters for the legislator in response to requests for information from his constituents. The staff's resources with their expertise of the pyramid's members outweigh any other educational staff resources available to the legislator. Similarly, feeding information and useful questions to individual legislators for use at hearings on proposed educational legislation can virtually "make" an assemblyman into an "expert" in his colleagues' eyes, thus enhancing his status with fellow members of the legislature. The legislature, as a whole, gains relief from confusing and conflicting demands when a locus for accommodation of interest groups in education exists outside its walls. One can hypothesize that this protects the legislature from militant groups in education, and, at the same time, adjusts and scales down the demands for legislation which might otherwise produce battles inside the legislature. At the same time, the pyramid serves individual legislators in another critical way. Legislators place the pyramid as a shield between themselves and their constituents when the latter ask for action which is unwise or politically unhealthy—they are given the opportunity of saying "no" without embarrassment. The pyramid can often absorb punishment which legislators cannot afford.

"There's no point in introducing an educational bill if they oppose it," is a statement providing legislators with an easy way out. The partnership implicit in this arrangement reached the height of a remarkable division of labor in California. During the 1940's and 1950's, the C.T.A. used state initiative procedures to get finance legislation by cooperating with the legislature while publicly appearing to go over its head. (This was not discussed in public but was clear in the interviews.) The relationship between the pyramid's leaders and the leaders of the legislature was not impaired by this. When the C.T.A. resorted to the initiative without having reached prior agreement with the leaders of the legislature, it violated a traditional social exchange. The hostility produced within the legislature by this violation is still present in the California situation.

Finally, a social exchange taking place within the pyramid helps explain the remarkable role played by the school boards associations in the prevailing pattern. Their active participation in the pyramid and the formal leadership office they hold in New York State's Educational Conference Board are probably not explained sufficiently by the professional cooptation documented by Usdan at the county level. The state associations' role seems too active for that explanation alone. It may be hypothesized that this vigorous cooperation is explained in part by some sort of an exchange made between administrators and the pyramid for "keeping the lid on" teacher groups.

State public school politics displays a structure of pyramiding associations including state associations of administrators, teachers, school boards, lay citizens and the state department. The apex of this pyramid allocates influence to school administrator organizations. School administrators seem successfully to have coopted the others, penetrating them from their grass roots to the apex. Rural dominance is constitutionally present in the several organizations and also in the whole. The pyramid's rural base of power is particularly useful and seems ultimately dependent upon legislative houses in which cities are significantly under-represented but where key committee positions are in the hands of rural legislators. The pyramid's activities have significant impact upon the legislative process beginning with the work of its intellectuals who formulate a legislative program in education. Viewed sequentially, this formulation is followed by the marshalling of information (made by research divisions) and the injection of the program into the legislative process. The role of the researchers and the organizational spokesmen, especially key elected officers and top level careerists, is most significant here. The mobilization of power at the grass roots becomes more significant as the legislative process moves into its final phases. Rural linkages between the pyramid's base and the legislature's election districts, capitalizing upon legislative seniority norms, are used most often for this activity. The traditional political myths supporting the system resemble sacred rural community values, specifically, being politically non-partisan, placing commitment to children and quality in schools above personal gain and achieving solidarity through a consensus framework, rather than through conflict resulting from clashing of interests. The system is supported informally by the legislature because of the social exchanges involved, especially those providing the legislature and individual legislators with the trappings of expertise. Legislators through this social exchange are not caught in the cross-fire of conflicting constituent demands for educational legislation. The position school administrators have in this system is reinforced by how effective they are at reducing the militancy of teacher demands upon school boards. Serious changes in either one of two conditions sketched above would wreck the system. The following hypotheses is offered for consideration. First, if administrators and school administrator groups (for whatever reason) were no longer able to prevent the alienation of state school board associations and teacher associations from each other, then the system would collapse. For example, if school administrators and their associations were to fall into disrepute with teachers and the public, it would be unlikely that they could function as the pivot of this combination. Second, if the rural linkages between the pyramid and the legislature were either to be broken or to suffer an overwhelming loss of influence upon the legislative process, then the prevailing system would first become ineffective and subsequently suffer internal disruption.

California and Michigan

The pattern which exists in California and Michigan is significantly different. The concepts of structure, activities, political myth, and social exchanges will be used. Since the writer has more detailed information on California than on Michigan, the former state will be used more frequently for illustrations.

The organizational structural view which the second pattern provides is one of state-wide associations of teachers, administrators, boards, and lay citizens without a single apex. The united front is missing. The social distance between these organizations such as the Michigan Education Association and the Michigan Association of School Boards is noticeably greater than in the prevailing pattern when measured in terms of links of customary interaction. Moreover, organizations not present in the traditional pyramid, which nevertheless have an effect upon the legislative process, appear. Becoming evident is "... the emergence of *strong independent* groups directly concerned with public school policy."[11] Not the least of these in California's case is the California Federation of Teachers.

The California Teachers Association's present structural problems provide a basis for study. Old cleavages and stresses which formerly were successfully glossed-over and "contained," now threaten the C.T.A. Specifically, proposals have been advanced for creating separate teacher and administrator locals within C.T.A. Similar are the proposals advanced for placing limits upon the number of administrator representatives permissible in C.T.A.'s policy making bodies. The urban-rural cleavage within C.T.A. is increasingly wider. The Southern Section of C.T.A. is harder to control.

From an organizational point of view, the united front is very much weaker today than it was ten years ago. Specifically, the restructuring of the state school board association's power structure in the mid-1950's ended that organization's cooptation by administrators and pulled it away from C.T.A. This latter organization's "bread and butter" efforts continue to widen the gap between them and the boards. In the process, school administrators and their organizations find it increasingly difficult to keep even a foot in each camp—let alone lead them. Efforts are being made to combine the different school administrator organizations into a single organization apart from school boards and C.T.A. A similar fragmentation exists in Michigan.

In connection with the second stage of the traditional pyramid's activities, no monopoly on information reaching the legislature now exists. With the Ford Foundation's help, the Assembly established a legislative intern program. Jesse M. Unruh, the speaker, was given thirty bright well-trained young men. Some of these effectively competed with the finance researchers both in the C.T.A. and in the state department of education for the attention of the Education Committee in the Assembly. This development helped make the As-

11 Masters, *et al., op. cit.*, p. 263.

sembly independent of outside groups when it came to obtaining information and expertise. George P. Miller, Jr., deliberately used A.F.T. informants in the Senate in order to break C.T.A.'s monopoly of expertise and information. This action resulted in increasing the Senate's independence of the old pyramid.

No evidence of the old pyramid's loss of ability to mobilize enough grass roots power could be more dramatic than Max Rafferty's election. Rafferty was elected by default, and incapacity of the old pyramid is readily apparent: the one-time pyramid could not agree upon a candidate. Election went to the primaries with three candidates, plagued with an urban-rural, north-south split among administrators and the administrator-teacher split made the candidacy of Ralph Richardson of Los Angeles a serious one. Richardson and Rafferty emerged as the candidates for the election. Ludicrously, the profession's spokesmen were cast in the position of supporting a layman, although a school board member, for the state's chief school administrator's office while opposing a school superintendent. The right wing champion, writing about what educationalists are doing to children, was a school superintendent, a member of the establishment, holding an educationist's degree. To say, "It could only happen in California" misses the point. The simple fact is that the old pyramid could not unite. Its rural structural links to the legislature were no longer strong enough to prevent hostile legislation. It could not pull together internally to support a single candidate for statewide office in education, let alone win an election.

C.T.A. is having a tough time maintaining a non-partisan appearance. To quote from Masters report—"But when the *parties divide* on issues that directly affect schools, the educational interests tend to lose their initiative; they are, so to speak, boxed in by the very tactics that in the past may have been effective."[12] In both Michigan and California, the combination of competition with A.F.T. programs and the independent (thus conflicting lobbying by the school board organizations) has weakened severely the state teachers association's appearance of disinterestedness. The lack of a united front has made it impossible to maintain the appearance of unity.

The new pattern characteristic of educational politics in Michigan and California gives evidence that there are strong independent organizations engaged in conflict for the legislative ear. The old pyramid is gone. The focus of pressure on legislation is now found

---

[12] Masters, *et al., op. cit.,* p. 259.

inside the legislature itself. In place of the political myth of sacred rural America, a much more secular public image is projected by these organizations. The traditional social exchanges supporting the old order are declining in value for those that acted between the legislature and the pyramid and for those that cemented the pyramid's member organizations.

State governmental changes preceding the new pattern.   One of the chief causes identified by Nicholas Masters, *et al.*, for the break up after 1959 of the old structure in Michigan is the broader conflict between the two political parties. "The problem is that this type of political atmosphere does not fully lend itself to the basic strategies of . . . non-partisanship, and low conflict appearance . . ."[13] Specifically, "The emergence of the Democratic party as a dominant force in state politics has been accompanied by a realignment of the major parties."[14] This has resulted in sharper partisanship within the legislature. Sharper still, in its impact upon education, was the partisan struggle between the Democratic Governor and the Republican Legislature. In California's case also, first was the rise of partisanship, then slowly, within the assembly throughout the 1950's and more rapidly after Governor Brown's election, forces were set in motion which the old political formula in education could no longer contain. This is most apparent in viewing the strong party discipline that is followed inside the Assembly. Here policy decisions in education are no longer confined to the Education Committee but are also made in the Speaker's office. Unruh successfully making education an area of political party conflict has gained political strength at the same time. The transfer of educational decisions to the Majority Leader's desk has made the rural seniority linkage system almost useless. The turnover of old rural friends of C.T.A., as the urban Democrats gained control of the Assembly, undercut C.T.A.'s position. For almost two decades elements of the Senate had unsuccessfully attacked aspects of California's educational establishment. They seem to have been regarded by both the state department and the C.T.A. as "irresponsible." However, when Miller and Hugh M. Burns emerged at the top of the Senate's internal power structure, many of the concerns of those "irresponsible" elements were found to be shared by the men who now control the Senate's policies in education.

---

13 Masters, *et al., op. cit.,* pp. 205–206.
14 *Ibid.*

Two recent federal decisions and their hypothesized impact upon the states.   It was said earlier that if the rural links of the prevailing pyramids (such as in New York's case) were to be broken or greatly weakened, the system would break down. The urbanization of one legislative house alone was enough to do this in California. Even granting the fact that the elected superintendency operated in both Michigan and California so as to accent the breakdown of non-partisanship, in neither case did that constitutional device so work earlier. If the Federal Supreme Court's "one man one vote" decision will break rural control of legislatures, it will almost certainly make the geographic structure and rural strength of the typical state educational pyramids dysfunctional—rather than just useless. Members of the present pyramid, burdened by the albatross of the traditional small town alliances, outdated by their historic non-partisan myths, outmoded by events preventing them from delivering their part of the old social exchanges, and out of step with the new intellectual universe will probably split apart before they adjust to the upcoming political realities. The Supreme Court's decision on apportionment alone would no doubt be enough to effectively destroy the prevailing pattern in many states. But this decision does not stand alone to this effect.

Some years ago in Scarsdale, New York, community leaders helped support the schools against book burning. A few years later, the education committee of the Scarsdale Town Club and other leaders in Scarsdale tried to change the educational realities of their school district within the framework of local control. That committee included men holding high office in the Ford Foundation, Dean Rusk (then president of the Rockefeller Foundation), and John Gardner of Carnegie Foundation. These foundations were supporting James Conant in his friendly criticism of American education and Harvard's School of Education in its national and international change agent roles. At the same time they were attempting to modify American schools particularly with respect to curricula and teaching processes. Educational Testing Service is linked, at its policy levels, with the same group. It too added its weight to changes in the curriculum by modifying its merit scholarship examinations *ahead* of the curriculum changes in the schools. The classroom changes resulting from these often misdirected energies resemble the mouse which the mountain proverbially has labored to produce.

One problem they tackled—the most expensive and least productive—was in urban education. Without hypothesizing a conspiracy, it is suggested that the Carnegie Foundation decision to support the study of educational politics, Conant's blasts at "the establishment," and Francis Keppel's dictum that education is too important to leave to schoolmen are not unrelated.

Hypothetically, the repeated failures to affect fundamentally the American school system both at home (through lay committee action) and nationally (through writing and financial support of ever larger though abortive projects) has led to the formation of a new establishment in education. This new establishment occupies the offices of education in the federal government. Its own published statements lay out its program. Ironically, it has gained public acceptance by the oldest political maneuver of deserting intellectuals—the charge of "establishment." Central to its program is the disestablishment of the educationists. A method for doing this is by forcing standardization of local education by means of federal aid and by threats of federal control. For this to be effective, replacing the old establishment with itself is a "must" but is not enough. To gain control, new offices of education must lift educational policymaking out of the local level to the state governmental level. The fifty states cannot be left each to go its own way. The federal executive's decision to put administration of educational matters in the hands of the new establishment (as federal aid to education begins to be a fact) coupled with the court's decision regarding state legislative representation cannot result in anything less than a revolution in state politics and also in the governing of education.

Hypotheses Concerning the Future

Certain general hypotheses can be offered concerning the future:

1. Political conflicts about school policy will take place at the state and national levels rather than in school board meetings.

2. As a consequence, the local school board's importance will decline. By 1980 these may be mere ceremonial bodies—a vestigial remnant of past government, roughly equal to what the county superintendent's office is in some states.

3. The *modus operandi* and secular philosophy of the power blocks with the conflict type of resolutions will replace the consensus building pattern. This may mean that the A.F.T. will emerge as the profession's leader in the political struggle. One must not underestimate the N.E.A.'s capacity to adjust to and operate effectively with the new political rules *in time*. It will, however, take a "palace

revolution" inside the N.E.A.'s permanent bureaucracy to accomplish this adjustment. If this adjustment takes place, one could expect young men from the cities to be the leaders. They would have the support of teacher personnel and of the teacher welfare sections of the career employees especially.

4. School administrator organizations will lose political power to teacher organizations. Organized, overt political action by teachers will sharply increase.

There is one area of potential social exchange in the political offing that is worth stating. Assuming the New Foundation Establishment fails to raise the tremendous amount of federal money needed to change urban education, assuming that the N.E.A. adjusts so effectively that the old educationist "brakes" are taken off the wheels of teacher militancy and political activity becomes normal for teachers, then one could expect a new social exchange between teachers and labor. Specifically, teachers, committed to labor, would provide a huge pool of *white collar* candidates with training at the masters degree level by 1980. This could result in having teacher groups become politically powerful.

CHAPTER V

Local Power in the Teacher Group–
School Board Relationship

FRANK W. LUTZ

School of Education, New York University

The struggle for power in local school districts as it relates to organized teacher groups-school board relationships will be analyzed as follows: (1) focal centers of power in the local district will be presented, and (2) some familiar patterns for dealing with subordinate organizational groups; (3) a model, found to be useful in determining power systems in local school districts and in predicting the direction in which that power will exert force, will be offered; (4) the organized teacher group will be discussed to illustrate this model; and (5) a summary will be presented attempting to define predictable outcomes related to the rise of power in teacher–school board relationships.

Focal Centers

There are three focal centers of power in the structure of local districts. (A focal center is a sub-system of an organization which is a center of power and through which one can see concretely the application of power derived from the power system. A focal center does not "own" the power it exerts; total power is vested in it by other sub-systems which are linked to the focal system.)

The board, the legal center. The first focal center is the board of education which derives most of its power from the laws of the state. In this chapter the school board will be referred to as the "legal focal center," even though the board is able to exert power not derived from the legal code. The often heard defense made by boards of education, pressed to share some of their power with other sub-systems, is that they are legally responsible and cannot abrogate legal responsibility. They will listen to but will not share decision-making. They allude to their status as the legal focal system.

It is recognized that boards have a legal responsibility they cannot, in the final analysis, delegate or abrogate. However, the demand for the legal process of approval cannot be construed as a legal mandate excluding others from the decision-making process. Even in the unlikely instance that a board might want to hold all decision-making to itself, it would not be able to do so. Teachers make decisions about homework assignments; principals set up lunch room duty schedules; and superintendents act on recommendations for teacher vacancies. In all cases, some review or approval is required from a superordinate. But many other than board decisions are made. Many times these are even implemented before approval is given, and in practice the legal right to decide does not require that all decisions be made by the school board. In fact, areas of delegated and shared decision-making are limited only by the desires of the board. Boards, therefore, should dispense with any argument that they cannot allow teachers or administrators participation in policy decisions because such is their legal prerogative and responsibility. The school board is likely to be the most useful sub-system to focus upon when assessing the total power system of the school district.

The superintendent, the marginal center. The second center of power is the office of the superintendent. While professional educators sometimes shun the image of a power incumbent, the role of superintendent is rightfully one of power. The superintendent who does not exercise this power is not functioning realistically nor as effectively as he should. There are many kinds of power and ways of exercising power; one need not be an autocrat to exercise power. As was the case with the school board, the power vested in the superintendent is not "owned" by that individual.

The superintendent has a major role in the interaction between the board and organized teachers. This role must not be one of deciding what the board should know on the one hand and the teachers on the other; nor should it be a messenger service, relaying information back and forth. There are those who advocate eliminating the position of superintendent from this interaction process. But how could such a crucial part of the organization's activity be carried on without a person in the organization who is highly trained and, in addition, is the chief executive officer of the organization's executive board? Such an omission cannot be defended, either by organizational theory or by previous history of practice in either professional organizations or union activity.

The role of the superintendent who finds himself between the organized teacher group (to which he once belonged) and the school board (to which he will never belong) can be defined as a marginal one—a person placed between two groups, holding membership in neither, and forced to interact with both groups. In one role the superintendent is the informal leader and the representative of the teachers; and, in the other, he is the leader of the formal organization and the representative of the school board. Such a marginal role cannot be played successfully for very long. To believe that it can be done is to believe that the goals of teachers (including their personal and welfare goals) will always be congruent with the goals of the school board. Even if both parties agree on the generalized goals, it is not likely that they will always agree on the specific goals or the exact ways of implementing these goals. This does not mean that the two groups cannot or will not work together toward a common goal. But in working toward the goal each will want to present its point of view as strongly and vividly as possible. If the superintendent is leader and representative of both groups, whose position will he support? Who in the final analysis will he represent? A representative of an organized teacher group has been quoted as saying, "When it comes to the confrontation, I've never known a superintendent who didn't know on which side of the table to sit." This person has not known enough superintendents.

Some superintendents do *not* know where to sit. There are superintendents who support the teachers' point of view, thus facing grave economic penalties to themselves. That is to say, a school board is not likely to retain a superintendent who does not support its members' point of view—nor can it be contended that they should. If the superintendent, the board, and the teachers acknowledge the fact that the superintendent is the chief executive officer of the board and must represent the board's point of view, he would be relieved of this "marginal" position as well as from the psychological, sociological, and economic dilemmas confronting him as a "marginal man." Then the superintendent could act more effectively as an educational leader.

The superintendent, who is recognized as the chief executive officer of the board, can act within the broad parameter set by a policy, once a policy is determined. Taking his role and acting between the organized teacher group and the school board in this capacity, the superintendent could exercise some important options. In this position he would support the board's position and the board could be expected to support his position. There is something revolutionary suggested here: that the board allow the superintendent to make important decisions when negotiating with an organized teacher group within the policy parameters, and that the board support these decisions without having previously approved the specifics. There is precedent for this type of procedure in the history of relationships between organized employee groups and organizational boards. There is no reason to believe that superintendents cannot handle negotiations as competently as company presidents nor that school boards can recognize the value of such a procedure. Moreover, because the superintendent is trained as a teacher, often has been a teacher, he understands educational goals and objectives and is more likely to understand the teachers' problems and talk their language than is a member of the board. Although administrators are often accused of not understanding the problems of teachers (usually it is claimed they are too far from the classroom), this is not the major difficulty. The fact of the matter is that the average teacher does not understand the problems of the administration, and the school board is not likely to be sympathetic toward teachers' problems.

On the basis of the above arguments one can see that, by freeing the superintendent of his "marginal role" and allowing him to occupy his role of chief executive officer of the school board, everyone is in a better position to handle the problem of organized teacher group–school board relationships.

Teacher group, emergent centers.   This is a focal center apt to be overlooked. Traditionally, local teacher groups have not utilized the power which they can mobilize. Occasionally superintendents of schools say, "We have no problems." The rising incidence of teacher union contracts and strikes, as well as professional organizational demands and sanctions, has tended to dispel what is a short-sighted view—that there is no present problem, no necessity for providing ways to prevent such problems.

To call the rise of teacher group power a "necessary evil" is a mistake. The exercise of power is never a mistake in itself. However, power is sometimes exercised for incorrect social goals. Teachers are not disposed toward anti-social goals. Sometimes there are factors which lead teacher groups to mistrusting and resisting administrators and school boards. This chapter will discuss how such situations develop and how a school district might *plan* to prevent such from happening. Since the exercise of power by organized teacher groups is the emergent pattern, the teacher is called the emergent focal power center.

Familiar Patterns for Dealing with Subordinate Organizational Groups

The rabble hypothesis. The oldest and least acceptable method of dealing with employee groups has been described by J. A. C. Brown[1] as the "rabble hypothesis." This idea holds that employees are self-seeking and self-centered and will not subordinate their own selfish objectives in order to gain the common goals of the entire employee group. In other words, each employee acts as an individual and confronts the organization as an individual. But since it is unlikely that any single individual can exert enough power to defeat the power of the total organization, there never is a problem in dealings with employees. School boards and superintendents who contend that they have no problem in dealing with teachers (and refuse to admit that they could have such a problem) operate under the assumption that the rabble hypothesis is valid. One cannot, however, contend that a method of dealing with teachers as individuals is a method of dealing with organized teacher groups.

Paternalism. An organizational head who consistently demonstrates his interest in helping his subordinates has difficulty in understanding why these subordinates sometimes desire to make decisions for themselves, without having first to petition him. This also holds true in some family life, in industries, and in school districts. Here the superintendent is always ready to sacrifice his position for what he views is the welfare of "his" teaching staff. He believes and acts like the organization is one happy family—his family. This type of organization is called paternalistic.

The head of this type of organization has a great investment in his paternalistic role; it is difficult for him to understand why subordinates initiate requests for modification of paternalistic authority. He considers them to be ungrateful. It is not a question of being ungrateful, however. As children become adults, as organizations mature, as organized teacher groups mature, they naturally will seek the right to decide issues without obtaining prior consent from the paternalistic head.

A mixture of the rabble hypothesis and paternalistic authority is

---

[1] J. A. C. Brown, *The Social Psychology of Industry* (Baltimore: Penguin Books, Inc., 1954).

exemplified in the statement, "Teachers who have complaints can see me. My door is open." Such an administrator intends dealing only with individuals. He stands ready to listen with fatherly interest, to give fatherly advice, and to grant requests with fatherly benevolence. Many a man who acts in such a manner is sincere, honest, and unselfish. It is difficult to criticize his motives, but it is impossible to laud his methods in the light of present social conditions. Actually he is heading for trouble and will have to face personal disappointments and discouragements in dealing with "his teaching staff."

The multi-group. Teachers and teacher groups make up a multi-group. It is not uncommon to have two or three organized groups of teachers in a single district each presenting the school board with demands, each claiming that it represents the teachers. Often there is no single group which can truthfully claim a majority membership of the teachers who are employed in the district. Even in districts which have only one organization and where that organization has more than ninety percent staff membership, teachers have not supported the organization even after it has obtained board agreement on teacher welfare issues. Boards have even been criticized by teachers for granting a request asked by an organized teacher group even though that group represented nearly one hundred percent of the teachers.

Yet, administrators and school boards who fail to set up machinery allowing organized teacher groups to exercise power (on the basis that they must hear all groups and all individual teachers, both organized and unorganized) are acting on a "neo-rabble hypothesis." They hope they will never deal with a united organized teacher group. This is the last position of defense for boards and administrators who feel they are defending their superordinate prerogatives.

What has been said to this point is a review of what has been and, to some extent, what still exists in some school districts. It is not contended that all administrators or school boards act within the stereotypes presented. As with any stereotype, the final picture does not look like anyone. Yet it tends to represent many. Certainly, the stereotype does not look like one's self. Nonetheless, one may see if anything meaningful can be learned from those presented.

A Tri-System Method of Viewing Local Power

The assessment of social power is high on the list of crucial areas of superintendent responsibility. It is a tremendous task for school boards and teacher groups who wish to be effective in an area where decision-making is essentially political in nature. The model presented here attempts to synthesize several approaches to social systems: (1) it enables one to make an assessment of pressures within the power system and a prediction of the responses of the subsystems of the total system to a particular decision, (2) it enables one to assess the state of the local power system at a point in the future. The type of assessment suggested here is necessarily related to a changing power system as contrasted to a static power structure—it involves a constant re-evaluation of that power system. The power system is mercurial and must be constantly reassessed for valid prediction.

The Tri-System Model is considered to be a logical approach to the assessment and study of local power systems. The Tri-System approach includes the theory of George C. Homans[2,3] which deals with the behavior of individuals in small groups, the theory of Charles P. Loomis[4] which deals with the behavior of groups with other groups, and the theory of general systems as illustrated by Von Bertanlanffy,[5] Hall and Fagen,[6] and McClelland,[7] which relates to a general theory of the abstract operation of social systems with other social systems. From the synthesis of these three ways of analyzing behaviors illustrated in Figure I, the study and prediction of social power can be expedited.

An application of the tri-system model. Not to make a complete analysis of a power system, but rather to indicate the application of the concepts in the model, a "typically organized teacher group" shall be used. In doing this, only one sub-system of the total power system of the school district will be examined.

The individual behavior of the members of the organized teacher group will be expressed in the three elements of behavior: inter-

---

[2] George C. Homans, *The Human Group* (New York: Harcourt, Brace and World, Inc., 1950).

[3] George C. Homans, *Social Behavior: Its Elementary Forms* (New York: Harcourt, Brace and World, Inc., 1961).

[4] Charles P. Loomis, *Social Systems: Essays on Their Persistence and Change* (New York: Van Nostrand Company, Inc., 1960).

[5] Ludwig von Bertanlanffy, "An Outline of General Systems Theory," *British Journal for the Philosophy of Science*, I, (August, 1950).

[6] A. D. Hall and E. R. Fagen, "Definition of a System" in *General Systems Theory Yearbook of the Society of the Advancement of General Systems Theory*, Ludwig von Bertanlanffy and Anatol Rapport, eds., (Ann Arbor: Bron-Beamfield, 1965).

[7] Charles A. McClelland, "General Systems and the Social Sciences," *Etc.,* XVIII, (1962), pp. 449–450.

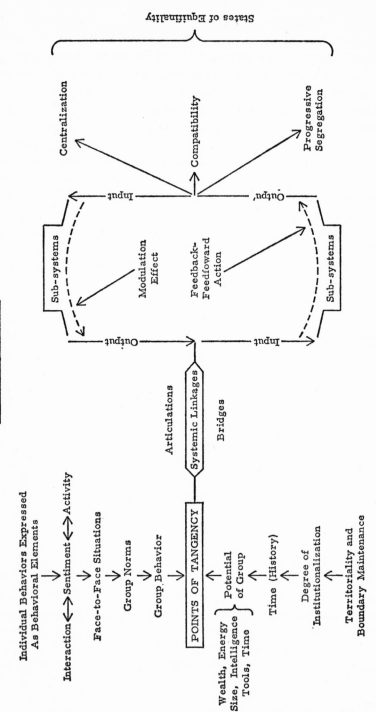

TRI-SYSTEMS MODEL

action, sentiment and activity. Most of the day, teachers' activities center on teaching and are influenced by environmental "givens." The assignment of a particular school, the grade or subject, the proximity to other teachers or administrators all are environmental "givens" that influence the operation of each element of behavior and the effect each will have on the other two. There are also environmental "givens" which individuals bring to the situation. These include: age, sex, marital status, religion, etc. These environmental "givens" will influence the elements and their inter-relationships.

"Givens" structure certain face-to-face situations. Naturally, teachers interact with other teachers who are in the same school more than with teachers in other schools. Those who must walk past other teachers' rooms are more likely to interact with each other than with those teachers whose room assignments are not on the convenient, regular path. The elements of behavior stem from such face-to-face situations.

The three elements of behavior are interrelated and the interrelatedness is easily demonstrated. The activity of teaching is related to the interaction of certain teachers. Teaching in a specific school, or a specific grade or subject in that school, further increases the interaction of certain teachers. As these teachers increase their interaction, they begin to form sentiments among themselves. They develop the feeling that "they" have the best school in the district and other shared sentiments evolve.[8] As these sentiments grow, the group often intentionally increases interactions among themselves, both within the school environment and without. Picnics, parties, and committee work are examples of increased activities providing opportunity for more interaction. When there is an increase in shared activities, interactions also increase.

As the elements of human behavior influence one another and increase, something else also happens—particularly in the area of sentiment. The group feeling of "we," which develops from the continued face-to-face interplay of human beings interacting, is one of the necessary elements for the formation of a group. Individuals seek situations where they feel they can "belong." Multi-groups, perhaps at odds with one another, can develop within a district or school teaching staff, but it is not likely that there ever is a "no group" feeling. The rabble hypothesis was rejected because groups

---

[8] For a discussion of activity and sentiment in a school, *see* Stephen E. Rubin, "A Social System Analysis of the Informal Structure of a School Faculty." (Unpublished doctoral dissertation at New York University, 1965).

do form, and, through the exercise of increasing sentiment, group norms do develop. The norms express the way the group feels its members should behave in particular situations. Sanctions develop and are applied to those whose behavior deviates from expectation. Without such norms no group exists. It is impossible for a teaching staff to have no norms. Inevitably, teachers can tell you how other teachers ought to teach, dress, talk and even think. Those who do not conform or "measure up" are sanctioned in various ways.

Individual behavior—interaction, sentiment, and activity—is expressed in face-to-face situations. It is modified by the environmental "givens" and results in group norms that provide the acceptable limits of behavior within the group. This group behavior is observable at a point of tangency. The teacher group is a point of tangency because it *is* a group and because it *is* linked in various ways to the total school system.

The lower left-hand segment of the model (Figure I) shows that the teacher group and the individual teacher have territoriality, both physical and cognitive. Teacher groups, administrators, and school boards dispute over who owns certain territories (i.e., who should determine certain kinds of educational policy). There is certain physical territory held by each group, but this is seldom at issue. The act of defending or attempting to occupy prescribed territory (called boundary maintenance) explains why there are disputes between teacher groups and school boards.

The degree of institutionalization of the group is often an issue of confrontation between teachers, administrators, and school boards. Does the teacher group have a constitution or by-laws? Are they recognized by school members as a group with whom they will interact regarding particular issues? Are there state or national laws providing for the existence of such a group? As these questions can be answered "yes," the institutionalization of the teacher group increases. Highly institutionalized groups are more predictable than groups with a low degree of institutionalization. This should influence boards of education which are considering the formal recognition of teacher groups and provision should be made for methods of interaction. The fact that a group exists with some normative structure provides institutionalization for the group. Institutionalization is not a dichotomous variable but rather a continuous one. The more structured and narrow the norms of a group are, then the more institutionalized they are and the more predictable they become.

Teacher groups have a history and are acting in the light of that history. This is an important variable in the determination of and in the prediction of power. What might be done today would not have been done yesterday and may be impossible tomorrow—for historic reasons. Public schools are as old as American history itself and are not likely to fade from the American scene. Good teachers are presently in short supply and this scarcity will continue in the foreseeable future. These factors play an important part in teacher–school board relationships, and the use of power.

The potential of the group is perhaps the most important variable in the segment of the Tri-System Model. It often is the most poorly assessed factor concerning teacher groups. What is the potential of the teacher group? (1) Size: with the exception of the pupils, they are the largest group within the educational organization, (2) Intelligence: all are college graduates, many hold graduate degrees, (3) Wealth: individually, most administrators and board members have the advantage, but, as a group, the teachers generally have the edge, (4) Energy: again total energy must be on the side of the teacher group, (5) Tools: here there may be a difference of opinion. Many persons, including the writer of this chapter, do not accept the strike as a reasonable tool to be used by a teacher group. Nonetheless, it has to be recognized as a strong tool which can be and has been used. Though the strike is considered a usable tool, there is the legal structure, the system of record keeping, the use of clerical and consultant help, all of which provide tools which could swing the balance away from the teacher group. Most school boards fail to recognize that they have these resources at their disposal. (6) Available time: here school boards and administrator groups have the edge. Teachers are occupied with teaching. The very job of administration provides time for action that enhances the power relationship. Total time, however, is available to all.

What has been said about the potential of the teacher group should not be misconstrued. The power that the teacher group can exercise (by itself) does not necessarily mean it must be or will be directed against the other two groups. This is far from the fact. On the contrary, the full power of all three groups might be directed toward the same goals.

Moving from points of tangency to the right side of the model in Figure I, the teacher group is a point of tangency in the power system because it is systematically linked to the other sub-systems. Taking the school board as the focal system (this is not only the most realistic but the most practical approach), one finds the teacher group linked in several ways. Several kinds of bridges always exist. All teachers meet with administrators and discuss educational problems. Administrators are often asked to report to the board on the problems that have been discussed with teachers or teacher committees. Thus, bridges are established. It is not impossible that teachers meet with board members in the community to discuss educational problems and this establishes additional bridges. As teacher power continues to grow, there will be more frequent articulation between teacher groups and the local board. This will occur as teachers become elected to school boards—there will be more articulation between state and/or national teacher groups and the local board because, more than likely, the elected teacher will be from a district other than the local one in which he teaches.

Because the teacher group is a point of tangency, is linked to other sub-systems, and is an open system, it will exhibit the behavior of an open system. It will exchange inputs and outputs with other sub-systems with which it is linked and it will use some of the inputs as modifiers of future outputs. This process is called the modulation effect. An example of this behavior: a teacher group requests discussion of a particular problem and uses regular channels to transmit this request. (The request is an output.) They receive a curt reply denying the request, or perhaps receive no formal response. (Either of these situations would be received as an input to the teacher group.) The group's next request might avoid regular channels and be sent directly to the board or even be disclosed to the public in the form of a news article. Thus the output changed as the result of certain inputs. (This is modulation effect.)

There are particular states of equifinality which might be predicted (based on data collected by an interested observer or a participant in the power system). A teacher group may act in such a manner that they gain so much power that they become the central sub-system in the school district's power system. The refusal to recognize the teacher group as a point of tangency in the power system of the school district will not prevent them from becoming the central system.

A teacher group, blocked from acting within the structure of the school organization, may continue to develop power potential and may become progressively segregated. That is, they may eventually become powerful enough to act as a separate system rather than acting as a sub-system of the total system. Teacher groups who sanction or strike against the school district have become segregated from the system and are acting as a separate system. Though it is impossible for the teacher group to become "completely" segregated, it is not impossible for them to become "progressively" segregated. The three groups, teachers, administrators and boards, can act compatibly to achieve common goals. Under certain conditions they will not, but there is no reason why they cannot.

Some Implications

Teacher groups are attempting to influence educational policy in a number of areas. School boards and school administrators take a dim view of this, but, in the long run, they will not be able to prevent it. The issue of teacher salaries ranks high but it is not the only policy issue with which teachers are concerned. One can predict that teacher groups will continue to press for a role in the formulation of policy decisions. What alternative courses will be open to school board and administrators then?

Centralization. School boards can do nothing or can do something. One tends to dismiss the option to do nothing as "no decision." The fact that a sub-system receives no reply to its output is likely to be viewed as an input and, therefore, will modify future outputs. If a superintendent or a school board takes the position that dealing with an organized teacher group is "no problem," or requires no action, no decision, and no response, the teacher group views this as a decision. Regardless of the fact that the decision is made on the basis of inadequate data, the decision to do nothing is a decision. The result of a decision to do nothing is similar to the result of a decision to resist the initiative of the teacher group. They differ in one way. By refusing to recognize the problem, one cannot resist the challenge for power effectively. By deciding that no action is necessary, the teacher group is told (by the fact that they are told nothing) that either the superintendent or the school board or both are not receptive to working with them in formulating educational policy. If the decision is to do nothing, the road is open for the teacher organization to act and to do so without resistance, except when confronted by established policy. It therefore mobilizes enough power to force the school board to allow it to participate in certain policy decisions. This seems a ridiculously poor decision to make but is made sometimes by school superintendents and/or school boards.

Left free to act but having no opportunity to act within the formal structure, the teacher group turns to the informal structure. Using sub-systems and methods which are less institutionalized and less predictable, the group will attempt to influence the decisions of the school board.

In the Whitman Case the following hypothesis was formulated:

> When the formal organization of the school does not respond to up-the-line communication in a way satisfactory to those who initiate such communication, the informal system will be used in an attempt to obtain a satisfactory response.[9]

Evidence from other studies as well as the entire history of employee-employer relations supports this hypothesis: faced with the decision to do nothing and thus unopposed in their action, perhaps even unobserved, the organized teacher group is driven outside the formal system. Then it is likely to be successful in its attempt to influence the board. It wins almost by default.

If the teacher group goes to the board through informal channels and the board reaches a decision favorable to the teacher group, logically the teacher group will use that channel again.

Several propositions taken from social psychology provide some reasonable predictions. Homans states:

> If in the past the occurrence of a particular stimulus-situation has been the occasion on which a man's or a group's activity has been rewarded, then the more similar the present stimulus-situation is to the past one, the more likely he is to emit the activity, or some similar activity now.[10]

Paraphrasing Homans' proposition to fit the exact situation:

> If in the past the attempt of the teacher group to initiate to the school board through institutionalized channels within the organization has been frustrated, and then after initiating through less institutionalized channels outside the organization they have been successful, on similar occasions, it is very likely they will again use the channels outside the formal organization, thus bypassing the administration.

Increased interaction and sentiment that may occur can establish social norms that tend to institutionalize this type of behavior.

Progressive segregation. Turning to the second option, the school board and the administration may decide to take action

---

[9] Daniel E. Griffiths, *et al., Organizing Schools for Effective Education* (Danville, Ill.: Interstate Printers and Publishers, 1962), p. 256.
[10] Homans, *op. cit.,* p. 53.

either to refuse or to resist the initiation of the teacher group to participate in policy decisions.

There is a good deal of similarity between this decision and the decision not to take any action. Both decisions can be interpreted by the teacher group as a refusal. This decision is different, however, in that the teacher group here has evidence of a refusal and they will meet organized resistance.

The board's refusal often is received with anger by the teacher group as Homans proposes: the teacher group views a refusal as unfair because: (1) they have had training which should allow them to participate in decisions about education, (2) they have served the local district long and well, and (3) as mature adults they have a right to participate in decisions which concern themselves. He said:

> The more to a man's [or a group's] disadvantage the rule of distributive justice fails of realization, the more likely he is to display the emotional behavior we call anger.[11]

If distributive justice means ". . . that a man's [or a group's] rewards in exchange with others should be proportional to his investments,"[12] then anger can result if teachers are refused what is rightfully theirs. Again paraphrasing Homans to fit a specific situation:

> If the teacher group perceives that they have not been dealt with fairly or justly, based on their perception of their own investment in the situation, the more they perceive the disadvantage, the more intense will be their anger.

The school board's refusal to allow teacher group participation in educational decision-making will undoubtedly result in some form of angry response by the teacher group. Again here, one can expect that the teacher group will attempt to influence decision-making through channels other than those provided by the formal structure. In this case though there is a difference. The board has decided to refuse and resist. One expects the teacher group to meet this resistance as they move outside the formal organization to the established informal sub-systems. The administration acts in accord with the board. As both administration and the board have considerable power, the teacher group finds it difficult to use informal channels that are established and controlled or influenced by the administrators and the school board.

When a strongly organized teacher group meets effective resis-

---

[11] *Ibid.,* p. 75.
[12] *Ibid.,* p. 235.

tance when attempting to influence educational policy, the more frustrated and angry the members become. Now a second road lies open to the teacher group: the teacher union which provides a channel outside the educational structure through which teacher power can be brought to bear. This is not to say that teacher unions are good or that they are bad. Rather, it merely states that the union provides a channel not traditionally within the formal or informal structure of the educational enterprise. Through it teacher power can be brought to bear on educational policymaking at all levels.

If a teacher group is given the opportunity to influence the decision-makers through formally established channels, they usually choose this method. As a second choice they choose to work through established informal channels. Only as a final resort do they look for channels that are not traditional within the system.

Another of Homans' propositions serves as a basis for prediction:

> The more valuable to a man [or group] a unit of the activity another gives him, the more often he will emit activity rewarded by the activity of the other.[13]

Again paraphrasing Homans:

> The more valuable to the teacher group is the response of the administration and the board to their activity of initiating to the board through formal channels, the more likely they will attempt to initiate through the regularized formal channels.

Conversely:

> The less valuable to the teacher group is the response of the administration and the board to their activity of initiating to the board through formal channels, the more likely they are to attempt to exercise power outside the formal channels.

Compatibility. If a board decides to cooperate with the teacher group in order to establish areas of participation and methods of participation in the formulation of educational policy, the teacher group will not be likely to move outside the formal channels. In such cases, the teacher group, the administrators and the school board could be predicted to act in a manner that will be compatible. Though this does not mean they will always agree, they will be able to work out their differences in a harmonious fashion and can move in a common direction toward common goals. This is the definition of compatible sub-systems. This is the steady state or state of equi-

---

[13] *Ibid.,* p. 55.

finality one hopes school districts can achieve. Such a steady state can be achieved with a teacher union, a professional teacher organization, or an organized but unaffiliated teacher group. The achievement of a steady state depends on the inputs and the outputs of the sub-systems, not on the type of open system that exists. Open systems that start from entirely different states can achieve similar or like steady states.

Assuming that local systems can act harmoniously and can "encapsulate" areas of conflict, what other advantages might result? This depends on what cooperative decisions are made by the compatibly acting sub-systems. There is one possibility that seems so unusual and so desirable that it must be explored briefly. In other professions its own members control (at least to some extent) entrance into the profession, and they set up sanctions, rewards and behaviorial patterns for those within the profession. For the most part, teachers have never exerted this force. By institutionalizing existing norms, control could be effectively and harmoniously achieved—a situation that was never possible under administrative supervision or board enacted sanctions.

The classification system developed by Gouldner[14] explains bureaucratic control. Gouldner has indicated that there are three types of rules used within bureaucratic organizations to control individual behavior and to achieve goals: mock-centered, punishment-centered, and representative-centered.

Mock-centered means rules and sanctions are imposed upon individuals from without and no one within the system has control over them. These are things which "nobody likes" but "everybody has to accept" or ignore. It is not unusual to see mock-centered rules in operation in school systems. These are rules legislated by the board, or perhaps by a union, without the participation of teachers or administrators (at least at the building level) and by these rules teachers' and administrators' behavior are supposed to be governed. Not infrequently both teachers and administrators agree to ignore mock-centered rules. The behavior of the principal and the union representatives in a school is sometimes explained by the fact that each acts under mock-centered rules which tend to inhibit and diminish his authority. Because both must operate under the rules of a contract that is negotiated by superordinates and which effectively restricts the decisions that each can make and sometimes

---

[14] Alvin W. Gouldner, *Patterns of Industrial Bureaucracy* (New York: The Free Press of Glencoe, 1954).

requires behavior with which neither agrees, it is not unusual for each (the principal and the union representative) to appreciate and respect the dilemma of the other and often close his eyes to the mock-centered rule.

The punishment-centered rule is agreed upon by one group in order to sanction another. The board decides to "dock" any teacher who is absent more than ten days in any one year. Such a policy is intended to sanction teachers who might stay at home when they are not sick. It is sanction-centered. The teachers develop a norm which may become institutionalized and if a teacher has not "used-up" his sick leave by the end of the term, he is expected to take the remaining days off. Thus, teachers sanction the board that "docks" them or does not allow them an unlimited accumulation of sick leave.

The punishment-centered rule must be enforced by either the teachers or the board, but never by both. It brings about high tension and conflict and is enforced by punishments. It is supported by the sentiments of one group but never by both groups. Such rules are a result of the sub-systems working in a progressively segregated manner.

In many school districts rules are either mock- or punishment-centered. Such rules are the result of sub-systems acting either to centralize their own position or to become progressively segregated. One is likely to discover few representative rules, for there is little compatible behavior among sub-systems. If this is true, to any extent, then one should consider the benefits of acting compatibly. Rules would be representative-centered, initiated by either or both groups and viewed by both groups as their own. Gouldner[15] says that in the representative centered bureaucracy:

(a) Rules are enforced by management and obeyed by workers.
(b) Rules generate a few tensions, but little overt conflict.
(c) There is joint support for rules buttressed by informal sentiments, mutual participation, initiation, and education of workers and management.

To claim there is no compatible action of sub-systems in school districts would be ridiculous. Curriculum development often takes this direction. Curriculum is developed when groups of concerned teachers and administrators work cooperatively, each contributing to the area in which he is best qualified. Each respects the other sub-system's "right" to initiate. Each usually initiates only where

---

15 *Ibid.*, p. 217.

it is most qualified. For the most part, there is little "overt conflict"; rather there is "joint support" for the revised curriculum "buttressed by informal sentiments, mutual participation, initiation, and education" of teachers, administrators and school board members. The fact that compatible action between these subsystems takes place in curriculum offers hope that it could take place in other areas. The benefits of such action should indicate that boards of education, administrators, and teachers would be well advised to explore the reasonableness of such action in all areas of educational policy making.

CHAPTER VI

Conflict and Its Resolution: Theory and Practice

BRUNO STEIN

Institute of Labor Relations, New York University

In the United States, as elsewhere, groups engage in conflict and bargaining activities. Bargaining, in the larger sense of the word, connotes an activity taking place between large buyers and sellers—economists call this bilateral monopoly. The process takes many shapes and forms: lobbying by farmers or physicians, negotiations between mayors and civil rights leaders, and collective bargaining between employees and employers. The process may be a loose, informal one, limited only by general laws and accepted standards of behavior, or it may be a highly structured process, carried on under particular laws, specific administrative machines, or traditional "rules of the game."

Concept of Bargaining

In this chapter the concepts of bargaining will be developed. Drawing upon the general theory of bargaining, how does one develop these concepts and apply them to teacher group-school board relationships? Much of what is known about collective bargaining in private economy and in public economy is relevant to education. Currently it is even being applied in education.

Teachers may be considered to be professionals in some sense of the word. However, they are employed by an employer. This characteristic makes them different from other professionals who, like lawyers in private practice, are small businessmen. Teachers are public servants. Collective bargaining is used by employed professionals in public service; this is not uncommon. The term collective bargaining, as used here, is not an endorsement of the American Federation of Teachers over the National Education Association. The term simply best describes the activity of a teacher group engaged in what the National Education Association calls professional negotiation.[1] While the way in which such a group bargains, the pressures it applies and the issues that are at stake may be quite different from a negotiating session between the United Auto Workers and General Motors, the theoretical principles are much the same. Another semantic problem arises when using the terms "strike" and "sanctions." Of course, both are methods of using power; they differ only in technique. Where sanctions involve a collective refusal to sign individual contracts, the distinction is lost entirely.

Applications of bargaining experiences. There are increasing applications of labor relations experience. Representation elections are being held to determine the scope of the negotiating or bargaining unit. Arbitrators are being called in to settle disputes of the negotiating unit and apply principles derived from experiences under the National Labor Relations Act.[2] Experts summoned by the parties, either to act as neutrals or as advisers, are often labor relations people. Names like Donald Wollet, Thomas Parsonnet, George Hildebrand, David Cole, Theodore Kheel, George Taylor, and Benjamin Wolfe are all familiar in union and management circles. The American Arbitration Association, whose work is concerned with commercial and labor arbitration, conducts representation elections. This trend is not astonishing. These are the people who have demonstrated that they know how to cope with group conflict. Their experience and knowledge could be transferred from industry to teacher–school board relationships.

The theory of bargaining. With this in mind, one delves into the theory of bargaining to see how it can be applied to teacher-school board relations.[3] To begin with, the essence of bargaining is power: (1) to provide benefits or satisfactions, or (2) to inflict cost or pain.[4] This can be seen when individuals bargain. Two parties can improve their positions by exchanging something—say, money for professional service. Each gives up something to get the other's commodity. If the terms of exchange are satisfactory, an agreement is

---

[1] James P. Steffensen, *Teachers Negotiations with Their Schoolboards,* U.S. Dept. of Health, Education and Welfare, OE23036, Bulletin 1964, No. 40 (Washington, D.C.: U.S. Government Printing Office, 1964), pp. 54–57.

[2] American Arbitration Association, Files in the office of Joseph P. Murphy.

[3] Bevars Dupre Marbry, "The Pure Theory of Bargaining," *Industrial and Labor Relations Review,* XVIII, No. 4 (July, 1965), pp. 479–502.

[4] Michael H. Moskow, "Collective Bargaining for Public School Teachers," *Labor Law Journal,* December, 1964, pp. 789–794.

made. Suppose, however, that there is an impasse. No exchange is made, and each is free to seek alternative sources of satisfaction. If either or both find no alternatives, the situation takes on an aspect of group bargaining. The economists would say that monopoly power is present.

When groups bargain, a variety of interests are involved. Leaving aside third parties, one finds: (1) group interests, (2) sub-group interests, as for example, where teaching and non-teaching personnel are in the same bargaining unit, (3) the interests of the organizations *per se*, and (4) the interests of the leaders and of the bargainers themselves. Thus, the outcome of a negotiation is likely to reflect more than the simple interests of the groups involved.[5]

Application of game theory. It may be useful to ascend to a higher level of abstraction and view the possible outcomes of a conflict situation in terms of a vocabulary adapted from game theory, since choices of strategy depend, to some extent, on the groups' estimates of the probable outcome of the conflict. One can simplify matters by assuming a two-person game in which the sum of the gains and losses to each side can be added up. Real life is more complicated, but the model will serve as an illustration.

There are three possible sums of gains and losses. The sum may be zero, i.e., the gains by one group equal the losses of the other. This can be illustrated by a simple successful negotiation that leads to a transfer of a sum of money from the taxpayers to the teachers. The real gain and loss involves, however, only that part of the increase that was obtained because of the presence of the teacher organization.

A second possible outcome is one where the sum of gains and losses is negative, i.e., net losses are greater than net gains. This may be true for both parties, as in the case of a prolonged strike where the ultimate salary gains do not make up for the loss of pay to the teachers. From a short run stand-point, this may be an undesirable result for both parties; in the longer run, it may favor one side if the other will, thereafter, hesitate to engage in such conflict. This brings one to a variation of the negative sum result: one side may be gainer, although its gains are not so great as the other side's losses.

The third possible outcome is one in which the net gains outweigh the losses. Again, one party can be a loser, but it is conceivable that both parties can gain. This last possibility may come about if the

---

[5] Neil W. Chamberlain, *Collective Bargaining* (New York: McGraw-Hill Book Co., Inc., 1951), pp. 239–282.

loss can be shifted to a group not represented at the bargaining table, say a higher budgetary authority that can be forced to rescue the local one, or by improvements in performance resulting from factors like higher morale, availability of better teachers at higher salary levels, more effective teaching in smaller classes, and so forth.

Dynamics of bargaining. Before examining the dynamics of the bargaining process, one must necessarily examine bargaining situations in order to determine whether or not they are stable. A stable situation here refers to one where the two sides continue their relationship despite occasional conflicts. Stability is possible where the groups have the ability to inflict costs on each other, i.e., where strikes, sanctions or similar actions are relatively premissible in fact, or in law. Stability is also possible where, by law or agreement, the parties resort to an outsider to settle an impasse. A third possible relationship, when neither of the above situations exists, is either unstable or else disguises one of the stable possibilities.

When the teacher group can merely talk to the school board, it is not likely to gain anything that would not otherwise be gained in the marketplace.[6] Ultimately, the group becomes disillusioned. If it breaks up, the bargaining relationship ends.

Contract renewals represent the dramatic side of bargaining. Shutdowns of any proportion, are naturally of public interest, and the threat of a shutdown makes good newspaper copy. In private industry, the overwhelming majority of labor agreements are peacefully renewed; the exceptions to the rule, having ample newspaper coverage, become the norm for the uneducated public.

Another view. The bargaining process can be viewed from still another standpoint: the presence or absence of built-in impasse solutions. It may be useful first to examine the process without compulsory conflict settlement so as to contrast it with the latter. It may be deducted from this that conflict can perform a useful function.

The three phases. Three types of demands and counter-offers appear, changing as the new estimates are made. One is the public demand and offer, by which the parties take their official stand and provide copy for the newspapers. The other two are both private. One is for the best hoped for gain, the other is the minimal acceptable gain. If these two private demands and offers overlap, then conflict can be avoided, and the success of the negotiations, from a peaceful point of view, hinges on the communications of the parties.

---

[6] Marbry, *op. cit.*

The solution will be located between the above-mentioned limits. The exact location will depend on the real and perceived bargaining power of the parties. Bargaining skill, which plays a vital role, includes the ability to cause the other party to overestimate the cost of conflict to itself and the ability of the adversary to bear the cost of conflict.

Good faith in bargaining is a vital concept. It may be said to exist when neither side seriously threatens the organizational existence of the other. The "rules of the game" in the private sector and in some of the public sector provide for this. The practice enables bargainers to take a more reasonable stand than is possible when one side is struggling for its very existence. It facilitates personal amity between bargainers and sounder and saner judgment on their part.

The best-intentioned bargainers may find no solution to an impasse; open or covert conflict can ensue. The choice of weapons used in open conflict is a function of such elements as the degree of militancy of the parties, customs, the *de facto* legal situation, and the strategy and tactics seemingly best for the given situation. The range of possibilities is so wide that only a partial listing is possible here: strikes, sanctions or other collective withdrawals of service; partial withdrawals or service such as refusal to perform extra duties; harassment, such as strict obedience of unworkable rules; requests to potential new teachers to boycott; specific political pressure; general lobbying; general public appeals. During the period of the conflict, the parties continuously re-evaluate their estimates on the basis of the observed damage they are doing to one another and are receiving from one another. The conflict ends when the private limits of both sides overlap as a result of the new estimates. Among the possible solutions is a willingness to accept third-party intervention in the form of arbitration, mediation, or fact-finding. Another possible solution lies in the destruction of the teacher organization.

The characteristics of bargaining where built-in impasse solutions exist are somewhat different. Where new contracts are involved, a variety of impasse solutions are possible, and stability exists when both parties accept them in good faith. However, the tendency is for bargaining to go all the way to the last stage of the impasse solving process, since there is no cost of conflict. If the impasse solution lies in arbitration or quasi-arbitration by a neutral, the side seeking alteration of the status quo will find that it is likely to get more from a third-party settlement by holding out to the bitter end. School boards will learn to give as little as possible during the negotiating stage. Arbitrators tend to split the difference. If the appeal is not to a neutral but to a higher level in the educational bureaucracy, the tactic of holding out may serve to bring the teacher organization into a bargaining relationship with the people who hold effective power.

Conflicts over the interpretation of an agreement are likely to have built-in impasse solving devices, such as a grievance procedure with arbitration, advisory or binding, as the capstone. The tendency to go all the way to arbitration is not as compelling here as it is in contract negotiation, unless the internal politics of the teacher organization compel it to prosecute every last individual grievance. Group interests do not lend themselves so easily to trading off and are more likely to be prosecuted all the way.

Seats at the Bargaining Table

The question "who bargains with whom" is an intriguing one in the entire field of public employment. In government, basic budgetary power is likely to lie in legislative or quasi-legislative bodies, which are not structured to engage in conventional collective bargaining, while on-the-spot administrators seem powerless to do anything else but carry out the mandate of the legislature of the city council. The situation is further complicated by the presence of several levels of legislative bodies and administration. In practice, the functions of legislation and administration are not fully separate; legislative budget makers are influenced by the needs of those who administer the program.

On the teacher side, the problem of who bargains *for* whom is the familiar one of defining the bargaining unit, long an issue in private employment.[7]

In the private economy exclusive representation is the rule, but many school boards prefer multiple representation. Under the latter approach, all teacher organizations retain a voice in the bargaining process. A variant on this would be the European type of "works council representation" in which all persons, regardless of membership, elect representatives to bargain for them. Finally, one must refer to non-affiliated versus affiliated teacher organizations; no doubt local independent organizations will grow, to the annoyance of both the N.E.A. and the A.F.T.

With whom do the teachers bargain? If our theory of bargaining

---

7 Steffensen, *op. cit.,* pp. 42–44.

is correct, bargaining must take place with some person, group or governmental agency that: (1) can be hurt by open conflict *and* (2) has the *de facto* power to make a settlement. This point may be obscured by existing official channels of communication and legal-political structures. For example, it is easy to visualize a hypothetical situation in which the following is true:

1. *legally,* the Superintendent is merely an employee of the School Board, powerless to make an economic commitment,
2. *legally,* the School Board has no budgetary power over the Town Council,
3. *legally,* there are no bargaining channels between the teacher organization and the Town Council.

When formal channels are absent, informal ones may develop. One can visualize a hypothetical situation in which:

1. *in practice,* the Superintendent's recommendations will, in general, be accepted by the School Board,
2. *in practice,* the School Board's recommendations will, in general, be accepted by the Town Council,
3. *in practice,* political leaders will participate in bargaining out difficult points.

No one arrangement is ideal. There are any number of ways by which the teacher organization can reach the group with power. Legal barriers to this can be tactics in a conflict situation. Since the teacher organization must find someone with whom effective bargaining is possible, conflicts over recognition and bargaining rights, and conflicts in the early stages of a relationship may be carried on for the purpose of reshaping existing bargaining channels. This helps explain why there are some bitter struggles over what appear to be minor issues.

Given a theory of bargaining and some analysis of the possible bargaining units, stability of a bargaining relationship may be expressed in terms of: (1) limits to conflict, (2) coalitions, and (3) accommodation.

Limits to conflict.   Conflict tends to take place under a set of limits. When conflict becomes institutionalized, these limits are usually well understood by the parties. If the conflict becomes intense enough, the limits may be breached, and a process of escalation comes into play. Escalated limits are difficult to reverse. To strike may seem like a drastic step for a group of teachers to take; yet after they have done it a few times, it becomes an ordinary and reasonable piece of business. By the same token, discharging tenured teachers may be an unthinkable act the first time it occurs. Hence a healthy bargaining relationship is not necessarily one in which open conflict never breaks out. It is one in which a reasonable set of limits to conflict tends to be observed by both sides. As will be seen below, there are forces in play tending to promote such limits.

Coalitions. Despite the fact that the parties to a bargaining relationship are antagonistic, coalitions are possible. The two sides may have common interests on certain matters. Examples of this might be the elimination of rival teacher organizations, or the size of the educational budget. Individual leaders on both sides may form coalitions against all or some of their respective constituents.

Accommodation. Once a bargaining relationship becomes institutionalized, the parties tend to develop an awareness that, despite occasional conflicts, they must live with one another. In this respect, the process resembles marriage: divorce is possible, but unpleasant and costly. As groups and individual leaders learn to appreciate one another's needs, the limits of conflict are re-enforced. This process may be disturbed by forces such as acute conflict, changes in leadership, and such other alterations in the *status quo* as technological change. To paraphrase Benjamin Franklin, nothing is sure but death and higher school taxes.

Scope of bargaining. The approach here to the question of the scope of bargaining is by classifying the major topics of bargaining three ways: (1) the welfare of the bargaining organization, (2) direct welfare of the teachers (and others in the bargaining unit), and (3) professional interests. These three major headings are by no means mutually exclusive and should not be considered so.

Some of the topics that fall under the first heading are items like recognition; definition of the bargaining unit; exclusive representation; the obligation to bargain; negotiating and impasse-breaking procedures; dues check-off; special privileges for representatives and the rights and obligations of the signatories to an agreement. Under the second heading comes direct economic issues: salary levels and salary structure, fringe benefits, sick leave, job security, transfers and promotions, duty assignments, class size limitations, working conditions in general. Under professional interests would be classified matters such as qualification standards and new appointments; the role and use of professional supporting personnel, such as guidance counselors, psychologists; technological changes like the use of teaching machines and non-professional teaching personnel; and last and possibly least, educational and curriculum policy.[8] Most of the topics listed under professional interests are closely connected with the direct economic welfare of teachers. High qualification standards for new appointments can do more to raise salaries, by restricting supply, than strikes or sanctions.

At first, the bargaining focuses on the direct interests of teachers and their organizations. Like all bargaining, this will involve some yielding of authority by school administrators. The scope of bargaining will undoubtedly expand, since there is nothing a school administration does that is not of interest to teachers. If teacher organizations prove their worth as professionals rather than being merely craft unions of white collar workers, then professional topics will appear with increasing frequency. It is too early to tell whether this will happen.

Looking Ahead

The temptation to discuss the outlook for the future is too great to be resisted. Like any economist's forecast, this one is based on an evaluation of forces presently at play.

There is a likelihood for increased teacher organization in the near future, stimulated by N.E.A. and A.F.T. activity, but not confined to these two organizations. Nothing succeeds like success. However, different types of bargaining relationships are likely to develop in different places, reflecting local situations. In many places, patterns of accommodation will probably emerge after some initial conflict— if given the chance to do so by an absence of hard-core resistance from state and local authorities. Some teacher organizations will be destroyed by hard core resistance.

The economic impact of teacher organization in any area will be greatest at the initial stage of the relationship and where salary levels and structures are most out of line with the relevant labor market for teachers. Thereafter, the ability of teacher organizations to raise salaries significantly beyond market levels will depend on their ability to alter conditions in the market for teachers. On the demand side, this involves such matters as class size, special subjects. The local demand for teachers is affected by the local economy, including migration patterns, as well as by local economic policies. Federal funds will have an increasing impact here. The overall demand for teachers is not likely to rise as sharply as it did in the

---

[8] Robert E. Ohm and Oliver D. Johns, eds., *Negotiations in Schools* ([n.p.]: University of Oklahoma, College of Education, 1956).

past—until the mid-1970's when the war babies' babies come to school. Right now, birth rates are falling.

On the supply side, teachers can try to restrict entry into the profession by such devices as higher professional qualifications. Factors affecting a local supply situation include the accessibility to schools of education and the availability of young unmarried women with education degrees and middle-aged ex-teachers. Despite the growing number of male teachers entering the profession, it is the availability of these women as a labor reserve that influences salaries.

CHAPTER VII

Board–Superintendent–Teacher Relations: Viable Alternatives to the Status Quo

DANIEL E. GRIFFITHS

Dean, School of Education, New York University

The purpose of this chapter is to present viable alternatives to present practice in board–superintendent–teacher relations. The chapters preceding this one were written by social scientists or by professors of educational administration with social science orientations. These chapters contain analyses of the present state of affairs, rationales for its existence, and projections of trends as now foreseeable. These approaches are within the social science tradition, but they do not offer any alternative courses of action nor do they present any new, creative approaches which might broaden the range of alternatives available to board members, superintendents, and teachers. This chapter attempts to move beyond present practice by suggesting innovations which might be appropriately used by the educational world—ones which might prove more successful than those retaining the status quo.

Probably no problem is more important nor more vexing to boards of education and administrators than the problem of relations with teachers. This problem has a special significance in the New York metropolitan area because of the apparent success of the American Federation of Teachers in New York City. The ability of the teachers union to flaunt state law prohibiting strikes by state employees and the union's success in forcing disputes to be mediated rather than being settled by collective bargaining have led many teachers to follow the teachers' union path. Even those teachers in communities which do not believe in teacher unions have revised their strategy and tactics within their National Education Association affiliated local group in order to adopt union practices. At the present time, there seems to be little difference between teacher unions and teacher associations when it comes to militancy, effec-

96

tiveness in negotiating, or in the vigor with which they pursue their goals.

The following document is a copy (with slight and unimportant alterations) of a proposed "Agreement" presented by a teachers association to its board of education. Most of the issues and problems contained in this document have, in the ordinary course of events, to be ratified by all parties first. A "contract" usually follows, in which specifics are itemized. This document points out in a realistic manner the issues in board–superintendent–teacher relations.

. . . . *Agreement* . . . .

THIS AGREEMENT IS MADE AND ENTERED INTO on this _____ day of _____, 196__, by and between the BOARD OF EDUCATION OF _____ SCHOOLS (hereinafter referred to as the "Board") and the _____ TEACHERS' ASSOCIATION (hereinafter referred to as the "Association").

PRINCIPLES

The Board and the Association recognize that teaching is a profession. It is further recognized that the best interests of public education will be served by establishing an orderly method by which the Board and representatives of the professional staff can discuss these matters. To this end, free exchange of views among the Board, Administration, and the Association is desirable and necessary. Therefore, the Board and the Association hereby adopt the following procedure.

RECOGNITION

The Board recognizes the Association as the exclusive representative of the _____ Teaching Staff for the purpose of discussion and negotiation on matters of mutual concern including, but not limited to, salaries, personnel policies, curriculum, class size, teacher turnover, in-service training, standards for recruiting teachers, and district planning, structure, and organization.

NEGOTIATION PROCEDURE

The parties hereto recognize that the Board, school administration, and teachers share in the responsibility of formulating educational policies and goals.

In order to formalize and facilitate such sharing of responsibility, a Professional Negotiations Committee shall be established.

Professional Negotiation Committee

The purpose of this Committee shall be to negotiate on matters of mutual concern.

The Committee shall consist of the superintendent and four teachers selected by the Association.

All meetings of the Committee shall be conducted in executive session.

The Board and the superintendent agree to furnish to the Association all available information concerning financial resources of the District, tentative budgetary requirements and allocations, and such other information as will assist the Association in developing intelligent, accurate, and constructive proposals and programs.

The Committee, or any group represented thereon, may call upon competent professional and/or lay representatives to assist it in considering matters under deliberations.

Teacher members of the Committee shall be released from school duties without loss of salary when negotiation meetings are scheduled during the school day.

Negotiations

Negotiations may be initiated periodically at the written request of either the Association, acting through one of its Negotiation Committee members, or the superintendent. Such request shall specify the subject matter to be negotiated. The Committee shall meet within ten days after such request and shall meet no less than once a week thereafter until either (a) the matters being negotiated have been resolved by agreement, or (b) an impasse has been reached.

If the Committee has arrived at an agreement with regard to a matter being negotiated, the Committee shall put its agreement into writing. Such written agreement shall be submitted to the Board and the governing body of the Association for ratification. If both ratify the agreement of the Committee, it shall be publicly announced and put into effect as official Board policy.

If an impasse has been reached as to any matter being negotiated, the Association may request negotiation with the Board. The Board shall meet with the Association within ten (10) days after such request and shall meet no less than once every two weeks thereafter until (a) the matters being negotiated have been resolved by agreement, or (b) an impasse has been reached.

If the Association and the Board arrive at an agreement, this agreement shall be put into writing and such written agreement shall be submitted to the governing body of the Association for ratification. If the Association ratifies the agreements, it shall be publicly announced and put into effect as official Board policy.

All effort will be made to reach agreement on any matter having fiscal implications no later than 60 days before the date for final adoption of the budget. The time limits set forth above may be extended upon mutual agreement.

RESOLVING DISAGREEMENT

If any impasse has been reached between the Board and the Association as to any matter being negotiated, either party may submit the matter to advisory arbitration by filing with the other party and the American Arbitration Association a notice of intention to submit the dispute to an arbitrator for decision.

The parties will attempt to select an arbitrator by mutual agreement. If they are unable to agree on an arbitrator within ten (10) days after notice of arbitration has been received, then the arbitrator shall be selected by the American Arbitration Association. The arbitrator shall be an experienced, impartial, and disinterested person of recognized competence in the field of public education.

The arbitrator shall make written findings of fact and recommendations of terms of agreement no later than twenty (20) calendar days from the date of the closing of hearings or, if oral hearings have been waived, then from the date of transmission of final written statements and proof to the arbitrator. The decision of the arbitrator shall be rendered to the Board and to the Association, and shall be advisory only, and no judgment may be entered thereon.

All costs and expenses of the arbitration proceeding will be born equally by the Association and the Board.

IN WITNESS WHEREOF, etc. . . .

The Issues

It can be seen that there are three major issues to be resolved. The first is that of recognition. Whether it be a teachers union or a teachers association, the particular group demands to be the exclusive representative of the teaching staff. In many cities this demand has led to violently contested elections between the competing groups. Thus the first issue is: Should the board of education grant to any one group the exclusive right to represent the teachers? The trend is for boards to grant such recognition. In fact, in many states (such as Wisconsin, Oregon, and Washington) boards are now forced to do so by state law. This trend is expected to grow and boards will be expected to grant recognition to a group which will have the exclusive rights of representation.

The second issue is: What is to be negotiated? Herein lies the major issue. (This will be discussed in detail below.) The documented "Agreement" summarizes the goals of most teacher organizations. They want to negotiate everything. In New York City this goal has apparently been reached and practically everything is subject to collective bargaining.

The third issue is: Who shall negotiate? The unions and associations alike want to bypass the superintendent and want to negotiate directly with the board of education or another source of power.

They want no intermediaries. In places such as New York City, where the board has no fund-raising ability of its own, the unions adopt tactics enabling them to negotiate with the governor and the mayor through mediators. In most school districts, however, the demand is for negotiation with the board of education. Boards are ill advised to accept this. In the above "Agreement" the preliminary negotiations would be carried on with the superintendent. This is a minimal concession boards can make and should be looked upon in that light.

There are two sub-issues which are more applicable to fiscally dependent districts, but which still have some significance to all districts, i.e.:

> How does one design procedures for collective bargaining when a board of education, unlike a business, has no funds until they are allocated by the city and the state?

If a board of education is totally autonomous and raises all of its funds by itself, this issue would not apply. But it does apply to fiscally dependent boards and to boards having sizable amounts of their budgets provided for by the state or by the federal government.

The second sub-issue is much more significant, since it concerns all boards that engage in collective bargaining agreements with the teachers. The "Agreement" calls for arbitration. Although there is a technical difference, the term might be "mediation"—as in New York City. With this in mind the issue may be stated:

> Does the turning over of a significant part of the budget-making function to outsiders such as mediators or arbitrators result in an invasion of the board's policy-making responsibilities?

In the New York City situation, it appears that the Board of Education has abandoned its policy-making function to mediators.

Background of the Problem

A review of the background of the board–superintendent–teacher relations problem helps find solutions that might otherwise not be apparent. Why is this problem so prominent now? One reason is that teacher needs are not being met. The blame for this must be laid on school superintendents and boards of education. Boards of education have too long taken the point of view that they must provide the cheapest kind of education possible in order to keep taxes low. The result: scandalously low and out-of-proportion teacher salary schedules, low prestige levels for teachers, a teacher status which is the lowest in the educational field, and a lack of opportunity for teachers to realize professional needs. For a considerable period of time, teachers looked to their administrators for leadership to help them meet their needs. However, this leadership never came forth. School superintendents and administrators feel that they must side with boards of education; the boards have not impressed upon their communities that salaries should be raised nor that expenditures for education were necessary to bring education to a higher level. Teacher unions and teacher associations look at this area in terms of dollars-and-cents values. Each of the four needs listed—salary, prestige, status and professional needs—could be alleviated by raising adequate monies in the local communities.

The professional needs which teachers attempt to get in their contracts (as is evident in New York City) center around such things as: (1) being assigned classes smaller in size, (2) having a larger number of professional personnel per thousand students, (3) being given help in the clerical and secretarial tasks which they are called upon to handle, and (4) being aided by non-professionals in handling such tasks as dressing children, watching them during the lunch hour, and the like. Teachers feel that if these conditions are met, they will become more effective as professionals. Since boards and superintendents have not improved these conditions sufficiently, teachers are now undertaking to do it on their own.

Another reason why this problem is present lies in the fact that chief school administrators have an outmoded concept of their role. Most superintendents, especially the older ones, view themselves as "teachers of teachers." This self concept was once true; there was a time when the chief school administrator was the only college graduate on the public school faculty. Frank Spaulding writes of this in his book *School Superintendent in Action in Five Cities*.[1] His first superintendency was in Ware, Massachusetts, where he wrote the course of study and proceeded to teach it to the teachers. Where this self concept still exists, teachers react to it with resentment and even militancy. The superintendent of schools must abandon this concept of his role.

The third reason this problem is present is because the board of education holds an outmoded concept of its role. Most boards place

---

[1] Frank E. Spaulding, *School Superintendent in Action in Five Cities* (Rindge, N.H.: Smith, 1955), pp. 46–48.

altogether too much emphasis on what they consider their legal rights and prerogatives; they also place too much emphasis on the authority which they feel is vested in them. Furthermore, most boards have not adopted an attitude toward the teaching staff which recognizes teachers as professionals. This attitude appears basically to have developed many years ago when teachers could hardly be considered professionals, but rather were either itinerant school masters or unmarried daughters who went off to Normal School and came home to live with mother. Boards of education must realize this idea is outmoded—teachers are now almost exclusively people with bachelors degrees, many of them have masters degrees, and many even, doctors degrees. Teachers today are highly trained and greatly specialized. The erroneous concept of the board of education as the chief governing board of a group of non-professionals must be replaced by the board's recognition of their role as the educational policy makers in an organization composed largely of professional personnel (even though most teachers do not now function as full-fledged professionals). Boards of education should look to hospital boards for guidelines of action rather than to industrial or commercial boards of directors.

People and Organizations

How can school districts cope with the demands of militant teachers for a new place in the sun? The usual solutions which business and industry have employed should be examined. This offers a first step but the aping of business and industry cannot help education very much. First of all, basically the organizations are different and, secondly, the people in the organizations differ considerably. Two recent studies, one by Robert Presthus, the other by the author and his colleagues, document this fact.[2] The first of these studies was done in large industrial, business, and governmental organizations. Presthus found that he could categorize organizational members in terms of their methods of accommodating to the demands of the organization. He used three categories: upward-mobiles, indifferents, and ambivalents.

---

[2] Robert Presthus, *The Organizational Society* (New York: Albert A. Knopf, Inc., 1962) and Daniel E. Griffiths, Samuel Goldman, Wayne J. MacFarland, "Teacher Mobility in New York City," *Educational Administration Quarterly*, I, No. 1, Winter, 1965, pp. 15–31.

(1) *Upward-mobiles.* These persons are the most successful organization members. The upward-mobile feels friendly toward his superiors and believes that they are friendly and sympathetic toward him. He has little difficulty making decisions in conflict because he accepts the organization's values as decisive. He is extroverted and gets along with other people, yet he regards his subordinates with considerable detachment—this leads him to make decisions in terms of the organization rather than the individual. Upward-mobiles enjoy organizational life, are successful at it, and reap the rewards of status and salary.

(2) *Indifferents.* While the upward-mobile revels in the competition of the organization, the "indifferent" refuses to compete for the organization's favors. Some indifferents entered the organization with great expectations but, being unsuccessful, reacted by turning their backs on the organization. Others coming from a working- or lower-class origin were taught not to expect much from the organization. The indifferent accommodates to organizational demands by doing his work, arriving on time, and leaving on time—but he develops his major interests *outside* of the organization. His anxieties are reduced to a minimum because he refuses to become involved in the organizational race for rewards. He separates his work from the rest of his living. As Presthus says, "He sells his time for a certain number of hours and jealously guards the rest."[3]

(3) *Ambivalents.* The last group, a small minority, can neither resist the appeals of power and success nor play the role required to gain them. The ambivalent finds it hard to get along with authority and cannot play the organization game. As contrasted with the upward-mobile, he places individual friendship above the good of the organization. When confronted with a conflict, he decides in favor of the individual as against the organization. His is, indeed, a miserable lot in the modern large organization.

Contrasted with people in the large industrial, business, and governmental organizations is the personnel in large school districts. Here the first grouping is very similar to the upward-mobiles of Presthus. About one in eight of the teachers fitted into this category called "GASers," a word made up from Getting the Attention of Superiors. Their activities concentrated on getting ahead in the organization: taking tests, doing all of the odd jobs in addition to

---

[3] Presthus, *op. cit.*

classroom teaching, and doing the things necessary to gain the attention of their superiors.

A category called "pupil-oriented," the largest in this study, comprised some two-thirds of the teaching staff. These teachers preferred to stay in the classroom, shunned administrative tasks or supervisory positions, and were interested mostly in children. Their complaints centered around large classes, in-school assignments, lack of visual aids, and the like.

Another type, constituting some five percent of the teaching staff, was categorized as "subject-oriented"—although other teachers called them "intellectuals." These were found in the specialized and academic high schools. More subject-centered teachers are in the natural sciences than in any other field.

The fourth category, called "benefits-oriented," constituted about 15 percent of the teachers. These teachers have only a mild interest in teaching, in the students, or in career enhancement. Their real orientation is to the benefits they receive from the system: vacations, extra income made by "moonlighting," short hours, or just the escape from boredom they find in teaching. They move about in the system until they find a teaching position which they consider to be a "good deal," at which time they settle down to reap the benefits. The benefits-oriented teacher constantly complains about salary, working conditions, or other injustices he can conjure up. A subgroup within this category is composed of teachers who are resigned, indifferent, or marking time. Some benefits-oriented teachers appear to have once been GASers who have wearied of the chase.

People in educational organizations then do differ significantly from those in other types of large organizations. Any automatic or unthinking transfer of procedures from one of these organizations to another is bound to create difficulties. What is appropriate for one is not necessarily appropriate for the other.

Suggested Solutions

New approaches to help in solving the problem must be found. Although something can be learned from the experience of labor and industry in their struggle over the past decade, there is not a great deal here to help solve educational problems.

National Education Association affiliates and American Federation of Teachers locals have been compared in cities where their strength has been approximately equal and their relation to the board has been similar. One study took place in Detroit. The list of demands presented to the board of education by each group were compared. If one looked at the list rather than at the title, he would be unable to differentiate as to which group had made up the list. Yet the American Federation of Teachers takes a rather supercilious attitude toward the N.E.A. and has even denounced the N.E.A. by categorizing their activities as "organized supplications," "collective begging," and characterizing one of the demands of the N.E.A. as a "right-to-eat law."

First, consider questions that relate to negotiations: who should negotiate and what should be negotiated? It is strongly recommended that all negotiations take place with the superintendent of schools and never with the board of education. The board should always be willing to hear an appeal or to try resolving impasses which come about between the superintendent and the representatives of the teachers. Board members are not in a position to know enough about the operation of a school system to be effective bargainers. This bargaining job should be reserved for those who have knowledge of the day-to-day school operations. The first premise is that negotiations should take place with the superintendent and never with the board of education. This may bring school districts some problems particularly with the unions and sometimes with the associations. But, if a board gives in and negotiates directly, it is causing itself a great deal of trouble.

A second question is: what should be covered in the negotiations? The content to be covered in bargaining should be drastically limited. Boards should never enter into collective bargaining on points such as class size, standards used in recruiting teachers, the number of librarians or other special personnel needed, or matters of this sort. Rather, collective bargaining should be restricted to salary, fringe benefits and personnel policies. These are "negotiable" and are matters that can be worked out between the superintendent and the teacher representatives. The board should always have the prerogative of passing judgment on agreements that are reached by the superintendent and the negotiating group.

The boards should do everything possible to avoid getting themselves in a situation such as exists in New York City. Mediators in the past few years have arrived at solutions to money problems and the New York City board has been in no position to approve or disapprove the agreements. Oftentimes these agreements have been reached in the early hours of a Sunday morning; they have been approved at a mass meeting of teachers in the evening; and the teachers have been back to work on Monday morning. The board had no active part in the decision-making process. It is doubtful that even months after the negotiations took place in New York City that the Board of Education knew what was "agreed." How could they know what they "agreed" to if the important decisions were actually made by people outside the school system? This should not happen. A board of education must set up a system wherein the board strongly maintains its position as the representative of the public and be ready to take the consequences for all actions in which it had a part.

How should teachers organize to negotiate for salaries, fringe benefits, and personnel policies? It does not matter whether they have a union or an association or some unaffiliated local group. This matter is largely up to themselves. Sometimes they might want to have a "welfare committee." They should determine among themselves the way they wish to organize, and then negotiate on issues with the board through the superintendent of schools.

Other issues, such as curriculum, class size, in-service training, and district planning, are matters of educational policy making. Each school district should have a structure whereby the teachers can have a significant and important voice in educational policy making. A Faculty Council can fill this structural need. This Council would consist of members elected from various teachers groups (possibly elected from each school building) or the members might be designated by the association or the union. This group would meet with the superintendent at regular intervals throughout the year. All policies concerning what is to be taught, the size of classes, the need for special personnel, the nature of in-service training as well as district projections and planning would be discussed in these meetings.

Matters of educational policy should not be written into contracts. School districts are notoriously slow to change and, if educational policy becomes frozen into the contract, change would be inhibited even more. Many aspects of educational policy now in contracts are efforts to remedy educational ills, but instead they are creating even greater educational difficulties. For instance, a policy proposed was: "No teacher in the academic high schools is to be assigned more than 125 students over a five-period day." This assumes that schools will continue to be organized on a five period day basis and that teachers will continue to be assigned a definite number of students; whereas, the use of Educational TV, or team-teaching or teaching to large groups might change the situation. School districts can become immobilized by writing overly detailed contracts.

Grievance procedures. All school districts need to have a recognized, publicly known method of resolving teacher grievances. This can be accomplished by means of a structural device, the written grievance procedure. The following is such a procedure:

Step 1. The aggrieved party submits written statement of problem or complaint to official building representative(s) or a representative of his own choice. Within two school days, said representative(s) shall confer with aggrieved and endeavor to resolve complaint. Professional staff representatives shall be selected by the Teachers Association.

Step 2. Written report of unresolved grievance shall be given to the building principal or the business manager (if non-professional personnel) within 48 hours after meeting (Step 1). A hearing is to be held within three days after hearing with copies to aggrieved, grievance representatives, and the district principal.

Step 3. A written report shall be sent to a grievance board of three especially appointed for the case by the district principal and with the approval of the aggrieved. Members of said special board may be teachers, administrators, other educators or non-professionals. The hearing of employee and his representative shall take place within 5 school days. Special board shall render decision in writing to all parties concerned and to district principal within 5 days immediately following hearing.

Step 4. A written report is sent to district principal who will render his decision in writing within 5 days.

Step 5. A written appeal is made to the school board through district principal who will forward copies of all previous reports of decisions to members of school board. The board will hold a hearing within 15 days in executive or open session as requested by aggrieved and his representative, at which time aggrieved is entitled to call on any or all involved parties. The board shall then, within 15 days following the hearing, make, in writing, a statement of the boards' findings of fact, conclusions, and decisions, with copies delivered to all parties involved.

In addition to the structural steps that have been outlined, teachers, superintendents, and boards all must develop new self concepts.

The teachers need to look at themselves as professionals and the schools must be organized in such a way that teachers can work as professionals. Superintendents need a new self-concept and there should be a new image for the boards of education.

New Self-Concepts

The professional teacher, a new self-concept. Beneath all the present day ferment, this new concept of the role of the teacher is emerging. Most public school teachers today are not professionals. They work in fully organized school districts, they work regular, assigned hours, most of them teach from syllabi which they have not prepared, and their decision-making is restricted to narrow areas. Administrators consider teachers mainly as interchangeable parts of a large machine—the school system. Most teachers now aspire to be professionals, to be permitted to make decisions on a wide range of topics, to determine their own personal teaching materials and content, and to be self-initiating in professional work. Teachers turn to the teacher organization to gain the professional status which has been denied them by the school district in which they work. In other words, they are seeking to have their needs cared for in teacher organizations since the needs have not been met by their school districts.

However the teachers are discovering that their professional needs are not being met by teacher organizations either. They are not being treated as self-initiating professional teachers in either the N.E.A. or the A.F.T. An example to clarify this point: the A.F.T. won a contract clause which gave high school teachers in one city a free period each day for the preparation of their lessons. Three teachers in one high school used the period to coach students for a dramatic presentation. They were reprimanded by the union because this was not a proper use of the free period. Possibly the teachers used the period improperly, but decisions regarding the use of a teacher's time should be made by the teacher, not by a union. These teachers now have two masters rather than one! Neither the A.F.T. nor the N.E.A. is meeting the teachers' demand for a new role as a professional.

The main reason why neither organization can meet this demand of the teachers stems from the way in which schools are presently organized. A school staffed by self-initiating professional teachers would differ greatly from present schools. Such a school would more nearly resemble a medical clinic than a present 5-day school. Each child entering the school would be carefully screened by a group of educational diagnosticians and would be referred to that part of the school which could help him in terms of his diagnosis. He would stay only long enough to demonstrate mastery of the topic studied. Instruction would be by whatever method was appropriate, be it teacher-tutor, a class lecture, a computer-based teaching machine, or a period of independent study in the library. The teacher's role would be diagnostic, instructional, and evaluational. Some teachers would specialize as diagnosticians, while others would be "general practitioners" fulfilling each function to some extent. The complex matters of recording student progress, scheduling individual students, recording daily grades so that each student's progress is known to all teachers, would be handled by computers. While automation may bring unemployment to the general public, it can help bring professionalism to the teacher. The school sketched is not so "far out" as one may think; a prototype already exists at the Systems Development Corporation in Santa Monica, California.

The professional superintendent, a new self-concept. An imperfect, but helpful, way of bettering superintendent-teacher relationships is to consider the dean-professor relationship as it exists in many universities. The dean regards the professor as a professional, working in a field which is somewhat unknown to the administrator. The dean does not view himself as a teacher-of-professors, but rather as a co-worker having a different set of responsibilities. He must provide the professor with facilities and materials with which to work, with money and space for research, and with time for writing and thought. The professor must be consulted about matters of university policy; other policy matters, such as admission and graduation of students are the exclusive purview of the professor. Professors and administrators sit together in faculty councils or faculty senates where they develop policies and procedures. In many universities, promotions and salaries are decided by faculty committees.

This approach is not proposed as the single solution. In fact, it is admitted that the relationship described has many shortcomings: changes are rarely made, much time is often wasted, decisions are sometimes made by those who know little, administration and leadership become difficult so that most deans do little leading. However, this is an approach that offers a viable alternative to the self-concept of the superintendent as a teacher-of-teachers. The superintendent should develop a self-concept as a peer of the teacher; he should begin to build an organization in which he and the teachers develop policies and procedures to recommend to the board of education.

Boards of education in new self-concept.   Boards of education must first reinforce the superintendent as the chief executive officer of the board. As such, it is up to him to administer the system. With full acceptance of this concept, the board should then assume its responsibility both for educational policy making and for evaluating what goes on in the school system. By adhering to policy making, the board would set up procedures by which the school system could function smoothly and efficiently, and also would make provisions for change. The board members would no longer be preoccupied with saving money, or solely concerned with business and management, but would be busy establishing policies for operating the school system efficiently. The term "efficient" is used here in a sense that all of the persons engaged in the school system would be working at optimum levels. Viewing itself in this way, the board would see itself as innovative, creative, and imaginative. Instead of attempting to hold down the creative activities of teachers and members of the administrative staff, such a board would be seriously building good relations with teachers, making certain that excellent teachers be employed, and, once employed in the school system, guaranteeing them optimum conditions for their work. The board would make certain that teachers become responsible partners in the making of educational policy and that the welfare aspects of the job be subject to collective bargaining.

Coda

JOSEPH J. AZZARELLI

Evidence shows the serious limitations educational administrators and school board members have in coping with crises in school management. In this volume Professor Callahan presented an extensive portfolio of these limitations. The story showing the effect of the scientific movement on school administration, the entrenchment of the depression years, the short-sightedness of the post-war boom, the frustration of the Sputnik era provides historical background for today's teacher association-school board relations.

It is not the purpose here to find fault with school administrators or school board members. Much of their administrative behavior and decision making abilities were circumscribed by social and political expediency, as well as by constraining local situations. In spite of many negating factors, educators have achieved remarkable goals. The record is impressive as Henry Steele Commager documents in "Our Schools Have Kept Us Free."[1]

Elementary as it may seem, it is essential to point out that conditions of life in the educational world have changed. School systems no longer are instruments for local manipulation. Public school teachers are no longer timid and self-effacing as in pre-World War II days. School administrators and school board members no longer hold the exclusive operational tools of power. In short, school systems are no longer closed systems. In fact, they have never been.

Even so, there still are many school administrators and school board members who fail to recognize the fact that revolutionary changes are surging about them; others fail to come to terms with changes even though they recognize changes are all about them. In the instance of growing teacher organizations, many school boards fail to realize that teachers can wield great power inherent in such organizations. In essence, school boards were not moved by the evi-

---

[1] *See* Henry Steele Commager, "Our Schools Have Kept Us Free," *Life,* October 16, 1950, pp. 46–47.

dence presented when national sociological studies were made nor by the "cold" facts shown in the United States census reports.

Assuming, as Laurence Iannaccone and David Selden do, that teacher unions will grow in number and in power, what can be done to prevent or diminish conflict, disruption, and misunderstanding among teachers, school administrators, and school board members? What training or other preparation can help develop new adminis-tive skills when teacher-administrator relationships are involved?

A spontaneous response suggests that in-service and pre-service training institutions include in their professional preparation such courses as labor-management relations, methodology of contract negotiation, labor legislation, and similar factors. In the short run, these courses will help in developing an understanding of the proc-esses for settling disputes in school management.

Most of these programs could be initiated in colleges and universi-ties with minimum difficulty. Such programs could be conducted as workshops, clinics, seminars, in-service training sessions, or as for-mal course work at colleges, universities, or state education depart-ments. Such experiences could help learning (1) through field studies, (2) by means of lectures and demonstrations, (3) by simu-lation, or (4) by mock trials.

In the long run, these training programs should become institu-tionalized in the on-going training program for educational admin-istrators at the colleges and universities where formalized and experimental studies can be programmed. The following are sugges-tions for such a program:

    I. Social and philosophical foundations of education including the sociology of the educational profession, the politics of power, etc.;

   II. Behavioral sciences foundations including the psychology of group relations, sensitivity training and conflict analysis, hu-man relations, power system analysis, etc.; and

  III. Technological foundations in the methods of resolving per-sonnel problems including economics of public education, personnel relations, labor legislation, methods of contract ne-gotiations, etc.

Groundwork has already been prepared in some instances for many elements of the program suggested above. These program ele-ments are drawn from such disciplines as political science, psy-chology, economics, sociology, and industrial management. These program elements can be adapted and refined for training of educational administrators. One can foresee eventual graduate school programs designed to train specialists in teacher union-administrator-board member relations.

In the meantime, short-term programs, seminars, and workshops can be organized for administrators, school board members, school district lawyers, and representatives of teacher unions or associations. These can focus on developing an awareness of the historical and social antecedents of teacher-management conflicts and on acquiring the basic social science skills necessary for dealing with the issues involved.

Increasing numbers of school districts will have to face the issue of contract negotiations with teacher unions or associations—that trend seems clear. Superintendent Santopolo predicts that, as in past crises, school administrators will welcome the new responsibility. In order to meet this responsibility with skill and determination, school administrators can follow two alternatives. The first is setting up an immediate re-training program where the skills and competencies requisite for effective bargaining with representatives of teacher unions and associations can be acquired. But it must be remembered that this would be a "crash" type of program which only touches the threshold of professional skill for dealing with this kind of organizational problem.

The second alternative is setting up a systematic training program for graduate students in educational administration. In time these programs will supply a core of professional negotiating agents who will work with local school systems or state education departments.

During the current teacher-administrator-board member conflicts, it is recommended that school districts call upon recognized specialists who are available to cope with these problems. Even though industrial-relations consultants may be unfamiliar with school problems, they can provide expertise in resolving these kinds of conflicts. Since these consultants have acquired the knowledge and skill required for making contract negotiations, they can provide the superintendent and the school board with alternative courses of action. They may not be able to provide "pat" solutions based on their labor experience because factors peculiar only to the education profession exist. However, it is possible that they can offer some helpful insights as well as creative approaches toward solution.

Selected Bibliography

BOOKS

Brown, J. A. C., *The Social Psychology of Industry*. Baltimore: Penguin Books, Inc., 1954.

Chamberlain, Neil W., *Collective Bargaining*. New York: McGraw-Hill Book Co., Inc., 1951.

Griffiths, Daniel E., *et al.*, *Organizing Schools for Effective Education*. Danville, Ill.: Interstate Printers and Publishers, Inc., 1962.

Homans, George C., *Social Behavior: Its Elementary Forms*. New York: Harcourt, Brace & World Co., 1961.

Lieberman, Myron, *Education as a Profession*. Englewood Cliffs, N.J.: Prentice-Hall, Inc., 1956.

Management Relations with Organized Public Employees, ed. Kenneth O. Warner. Chicago: Public Personnel Association, 1963.

Ohm, Robert E., and William G. Monahan, "Power and Stress in Organizational Response to Collective Action," in *The Superintendent Confronts Collective Action*, eds. Robert E. Ohm and Oliver D. Johns. Norman: University of Oklahoma, 1965.

Selznick, Philip, *TVA and the Grass Roots*. Berkeley: University of California Press, 1949.

Walton, Richard E., and Robert B. McKersie, *A Behavioral Theory of Labor Negotiations*. New York: McGraw-Hill Book Co., Inc., 1965.

ARTICLES

Becker, Harry A., "The Role of School Administrators in Professional Negotiations," *American School Board Journal*, CL, No. 5 (May, 1965).

Bruce, W. C., "Illegal Strike," *American School Board Journal*, CXLIV (January, 1962).

Carr, William G., "The Assault on Professional Independence," *Phi Delta Kappan*, XLVI, No. 1 (September, 1964).

Cogen, Charles, "The State of the Union," Address delivered to the 49th Annual Convention of the American Federation of Teachers, Los Angeles (August 23, 1965).

Corey, A. F., "Why Teacher Strikes Must be Rejected by the Profession and Why Sanction Should be Considered," *Nations Schools*, LXX (September, 1963).

Educational Policies Commission of the NEA and AASA, "The Public Interest in How Teachers Organize," *NEA Journal*, LIII, No. 6 (September, 1964).

Elam, Stanley, "Who's Ahead and Why—The NEA-AFT Rivalry," *Phi Delta Kappan*, XLVI, No. 1 (September, 1964).

Gross, Calvin, "Ways to Deal with the New Teacher Militancy," *Phi Delta Kappan*, XLVI, No. 4 (December, 1964).

Lewis, Edmund L., "Collective Negotiations—Present and Future," *California School Boards*, XXIV, No. 7 (July-August, 1965).

Lieberman, Myron, "Teacher Strikes: Acceptable Strategy," *Phi Delta Kappan*, XLVI, No. 6 (February, 1965).

———, "Who Speaks for Teachers?" *Saturday Review*, XLVIII, No. 25 (June 19, 1965).

Lutz, Frank W., "Power Structure Theory and School Board Decision Making Process," *Educational Theory,* I (January, 1965).

Marbry, Bevars Dupre, "The Pure Theory of Bargaining," *Industrial and Labor Relations Review,* XVIII, No. 4 (July, 1965).

McCarty, Donald J., and Vincent C. Nuccio, "How Good are Personnel Relationships in New York?" Albany: Council for Administrative Leadership (1964).

Megel, C. J., "Can a Case be Made for Teachers' Unions?" *Nations Schools,* LXXIII, (September, 1964).

―――, "Teacher Conscription―Basis of Association Membership?" *Teachers College Record,* LXVI, No. 2 (October, 1964).

Moskow, Michael H., "Collective Bargaining for Public School Teachers," *Labor Law Journal,* (December, 1964).

National Education Association. Research Division, "Professional Negotiation with School Boards: A Legal Analysis and Review." Washington, D.C.: NEA (School Law Series, Research Report 1965).

―――, "Professional Negotiation: Selected Statements of School Board, Administrator, Teacher Relationships." Rev. ed. Washington, D.C.: NEA (February, 1964).

National School Boards Association, "A Report and Source Book on Board-Administrator-Teacher Relations: Providing Equal Education Opportunity, Long Range Goals NSBA," Delegate Assembly Workshop of the NSBA, Evanston, Illinois: NSBA, (1964).

"Negotiations with Teachers," *Theory Into Practice,* IV, No. 2 (April, 1965).

New Jersey State Federation of Boards of Education, *The Need for Balance: A Second Report on Board-Superintendent-Staff Relationships,* Trenton: The Federation, (1965).

―――, *1965 Legislative Goals.* Trenton: The Federation. (1965.)

Seitz, Reynolds C., "Rights of Public School Teachers to Engage in Collective Bargaining and Other Concerted Activities," *1963 Yearbook of School Law,* Danville, Ill.: The Interstate Printers, 1963.

Selden, David, "American Federation of Teachers: What it Wants, How it Bargains, Where it is Headed," *Scholastic,* VIII, (Fall, 1964).

Steffensen, James P., "Three Keys to Compromise," *Pennsylvania School Boards Association Bulletin,* XXIX, No. 1 (March, 1965).

Stiles, Lindley J., "Ideas from Abroad for Winning Teacher Loyalty," *Phi Delta Kappan,* XLV, No. 6 (March, 1964).

Stinnett, T. M., "Professional Negotiations, Collective Bargaining, Sanctions and Strikes, *School Personnel Bulletin,* XLVIII, (April, 1964).

Stewart, M., and J. Rynn, "Airing the Issue Concerning the Rights and Obligations of Teachers to Negotiate," *Instructor,* LXXIII, (February, 1964).

Street, Marion L., "Professional Associations―More than Unions," *Teachers College Record,* LXVI, No. 3 (December, 1964).

"Teachers Right to Strike," *School and Society.* XCII, (March, 1964).

West, Allan M., "Professional Negotiations or Collective Bargaining?" *The National Elementary Principal,* XLII, No. 4 (November, 1965).

Wildman, Wesley A., "Collective Action by Public School Teachers," *Industrial and Labor Relations Review,* XVIII, No. 1 (October, 1964).

―――, "Collective Action by Public School Teachers: An Emerging Issue," *Administrator's Notebook,* XI, No. 6 (February, 1963).

Wynn, Richard, "An Inept Lesson in Educational Policy-Making," *Phi Delta Kappan,* XLVI, No. 6 (February, 1965).

Index